I FORGIVE

*The Words That Can Transform
Your Life,
Regardless of Circumstances*

Sunnee K. Roman

About This Image:

Known as The Golden Section or as The Divine Proportion, this image is based upon a proportional formula that dates back at least 2,000 years. The properties of The Golden Section are found in nature, art, music, and mathematics.

The proportions of The Golden Section can be found in the Egyptian pyramids and within Greek architecture. It was used by Renaissance artists such as Leonardo da Vinci. It appears in the design of the Notre Dame Cathedral in Paris. The Golden Section is reflected in the proportions of the human body.

The Golden Section image has been used by most cultures throughout history. This image has an underlying presence in all of nature and all of creation. The author thinks of it as an image that celebrates the primary divine truth that connects all things and all peoples.

A How-To Book
Using a Unique Writing
Process That Restores
Peace of Mind

The Facts Are Revealed

The Actions Necessary
Will Be Made Known

Circumstances Will Improve

DEDICATION

I acknowledge, thank, and dedicate this work to the God/dess, the Ever-abiding Consciousness present in all life everywhere, the Oneness.

This book is also dedicated to all peoples everywhere, especially those who feel trapped, pushed to their limits, or who just have extreme life challenges yet who still have faith that there is an answer for them. This book offers a simple, unique process by which answers can be found, bringing peace of mind regardless of circumstances.

A special dedication and recognition goes to sole providers—those single parents—and their children worldwide. The importance of nurturing our future generations cannot be emphasized enough. Thus, it is a honor and a privilege to make a positive impact for those who need it most, whether it be locally, nationally, and/or internationally. For each copy of *I Forgive* that readers purchase, a portion will be donated to the Heifer International Foundation.

Heifer International Foundation
1015 Louisiana Street
P.O. Box 727, Little Rock, AR 72203
T: 888.422.1161
E-mail: foundation@heifer.org
Website: www.Heifer.org

"Every problem reflects an unforgiveness."

—Marianne Williamson

"Life is an adventure in forgiveness."

—Norman Cousins

"When one door closes another door opens; but we so often look so long and so regretfully upon the closed door, that we do not see the ones which open for us."

—Alexander Graham Bell

CONTENTS

"Do you want peace? Forgiveness offers it. Do you want happiness, a quiet mind, a certainty of purpose, and a sense of worth and beauty that transcends the world? Do you want care and safety, and the warmth of sure protection always? Do you want a quietness that cannot be disturbed, a gentleness that never can be hurt, a deep, abiding comfort, and a rest so perfect it can never be upset?

All this forgiveness offers you. . . ."

—A Course in Miracles

INTRODUCTION

Life is a process.

A reminder of this fact comes from the Renaissance master Michelangelo, who said, "I am still learning." To continue growing, evolving, shifting, adjusting, and "shedding skin" means to go with the flow of life. Mother Nature, our great teacher, is in perpetual change. Becoming aware of the moon's cycles, recognizing the ocean's tides, and recording the march of seasons from spring to winter is a statement of this truth. History has repeatedly reminded us of this change in the movement of peoples, cultures, ideas, animals, and objects.

To continue to learn, to be an evolved human being, does not mean we cannot be satisfied with our lives in the present moment. Radiating an inner glow of satisfaction, knowing how far we have come in our personal growth and development, is also part of the process.

Yet taking time out and taking time off from the treadmill of life gives us permission to review and reflect, to explore what possibly is no longer serving our highest good. Such things as repressed emotions, resentments, bitterness, grudges, blaming, and old hurts can be signs of a life not in balance and one that is blocking us from our greatest joy.

These things bring us to the subject of this book, forgiveness.

Applying forgiveness simply means never becoming stagnant in our lives. Forgiveness empowers us to make necessary adjustments, whether it be in our physical, mental, emotional, spiritual, or financial lives. Forgiveness creates greater freedom by erasing unresolved and painful issues. When we give ourselves permission to release old hurts or emotional blockages, we can free our inner spirits to soar. The empowering forgiveness process outlined in this book transforms ordinary people into extraordinary people. It will not matter your age, your color, your social status, your education, your country, your sex, your religion, your income, nor your history to receive results.

Forgiveness, the act of reconciliation, is profound. It is no accident that this book has found its way into your hands. The questions to ask yourself: Is now the time to let yourself or someone else "off the hook"? If not now, when?

I applaud and support you as you decide to take this journey of personal exploration and discovery to live in greater authenticity by unveiling the genuine you.

Life is a process. Live well.
...Sunnee K. Roman

CHAPTER 1

DEFINING FORGIVENESS

What is the definition of forgiveness?

The *New Oxford English Dictionary* defines the term forgiveness as: "Forgiveness is to stop feeling angry or resentful towards someone for an offence, flaw, or mistake."

The definition of forgiveness as defined in this book is: "An act of giving permission for positive and creative energy to reenter a situation. All involved are afforded the opportunity to return to a positive flow of life."

Forgiveness is further defined as:

- A powerful eraser of pain.
- The act of dissolving and releasing negative feelings (such as anger, bitterness, or resentment, etc.) toward a person or oneself for an offence, flaw, or mistake.

- The putting down, setting aside, cancelling, or letting go of a grievance and a desire to punish another or oneself.

- An inner process to remove any unhappy condition of mind, body, spirit, or affairs.

- A clearing of any negative emotion, a healing remedy, and an emotional salve for wounds by removing, relieving, rectifying, restoring, and renewing oneself. It releases the emotional connection one has to a person or situation.

- A process that is capable of cutting the ties that bind, allowing one to be set free from any person, place, or situation that may no longer serve him or her in a healthy and constructive manner.

Where can a person find information on forgiveness?

Traditionally, forgiveness appears to be mentioned in every global religion, New Age spiritual teachings, International Twelve-Step programs, self-help awareness processes, and by authors of numerous publications. It is not an accident that the theme of forgiveness is the common thread that weaves among humans everywhere.

What are some of the major, motivating factors for people to learn, understand, or practice forgiveness?

Not forgiving is truly toxic to the body, mind, and spirit. Holding onto old grudges, hurts, and pain is like drinking poison and expecting someone else to die.

People who hold onto their grudges, hurts, and pains can feel trapped in their situation. They are blocked and unable to see a logical solution to their circumstance. They can be in fear of possible consequences, feeling stuck and helpless with no apparent way out.

The Act of Forgiving Is a Choice

Forgiveness offers a way out. People can liken the act of forgiveness to that of holding a golden key that will empower them to unlock doors of opportunity that they previously perceived as being inaccessible to them.

Whenever people come to the realization that they want to make a change in any area of their lives, then forgiveness is a positive way to begin.

Benefits of Choosing to Forgive:

- Clarity: It allows the facts that surround the situation to surface.

- Freedom: It dissolves circumstances that no longer serve one's highest and best interest.

- Peace of mind: It brings the sense that one can live his or her life with greater joy regardless of the circumstances.

- Higher self-esteem: It propels one to move forward in life by releasing excessive emotional baggage.

- Results: It improves situations and circumstances.

- Empathy: It fosters greater compassion for oneself and others.

- Hope: It helps you recognize that you now have the opportunity for a better future.

- Confidence: It empowers you to no longer live as a victim in troubling situations.

If one desires greater peace of mind and the sense of freedom, then forgiveness is an avenue by which to reclaim it.

Forgiveness is an internal process that enables one to take an honest personal inventory of how he or she is really feeling about any given situation. You cannot change that which you do not acknowledge. As humans, we can choose to practice personal maintenance by "letting go" of any actions, thoughts, or deeds that no longer serve us in a positive way.

Forgiving allows us to let go of our emotional attachment to whatever situation is occurring so we can take back our personal power and move forward in our lives with greater ease!

Choosing to forgive is a very bold and courageous decision that sets a person free of emotional bondage. A person is able to release his or her emotional attachment to situations and outcomes.

In the following chapters discover how to implement this simple process!

CHAPTER ONE SUMMARY

- Forgiveness is a powerful eraser of upsetting emotions and/or memories.

- Forgiveness is an internal process that has the possibility to shift and/or remove from our existence any unhappy condition of the mind, body, spirit, or affairs.

- Holding onto negative thoughts and feelings, whether consciously or unconsciously, can poison our own lives and affairs.

- By the act of forgiving, we release attachments to the outcome, setting the foundation for magic and miracles to occur in our lives.

"He who angers you, conquers you."

—Elizabeth Kenny

CHAPTER 2

IS THIS FORGIVENESS PROCESS FOR YOU?

Jack Canfield, author of the *Chicken Soup for the Soul* books, says in the recent popular movie *The Secret* that most psychologists believe that 85 percent of families are dysfunctional. This affects approximately forty million people in the United States alone! Do you think some of them could benefit from understanding forgiveness?

The uncomfortable feelings we all encounter are what the famous scientist Carl Jung called the "shadow" side of our personal histories and psyches. We cannot skip this crucial step of owning our "dark side," which could be anger, fear, resentment, helplessness, guilt, or shame. We as human beings have a right to acknowledge whatever we are feeling. Forgiveness does not sweep our emotions under the carpet, but it does help us to neutralize our emotional attachment, "the sting," so to speak, that surrounds the situation.

Pause and reflect. Take a few deep, relaxing breaths, and ask yourself the following questions.

These questions will help you to recognize if you have in your life a need to forgive.

- Do you find yourself getting angry each time you think of a certain person or circumstance?
- Do you feel a sense of shame, guilt, or regret regarding your past actions or inactions?
- Do you replay an injustice over and over again in your mind?
- Do you want revenge? Do you consider getting even or settling the score with others?
- Do you make it a point to steer clear of, or avoid talking with, someone?
- Do you tell your story of what happened over and over again?
- Are you fixated on a certain outcome?
- Are your expectations being unfulfilled and leading to disappointments?

If you answered yes to one or more of these questions, it could indicate that forgiveness is in order. We must give ourselves permission to admit that we have been hurt. This is what it means to be human. This is such a necessary step because we are entitled to feel our feelings. We need to acknowledge what has happened so we can move forward. We cannot transform what we do not acknowledge.

All human emotions follow a natural progression. First, the emotion will emerge. Through time, the emotion will intensify until it reaches its peak. The progression will be completed when the emotion diminishes of its own accord. Unfortunately, many people interrupt this natural cycle of letting go by suppressing or stuffing negative feelings inside, pretending the feelings are not there, pretending the situation never happened. People have a tendency to judge or label their feelings as bad or unacceptable because they do not want their emotions to escalate out of control. By judging and thus creating this attachment to their emotions, they interrupt the natural process of letting go and quite often suppress them.

At some point, it is healthy for people to go back and discover the underlying causes of these suppressed emotions. Forgiveness is a way of revealing these underlying causes and so helps the release of the blocked emotions.

Thus, an honest assessment of how they are feeling allows people to uncover any concealed emotions. Add to this the intention to liberate the underlying causes of the negative emotions in a constructive manner, and they will ultimately set themselves free.

Does Your "Label" Work for You?

The glory of true forgiveness is that it allows people to stop being perpetually focused on unfinished business or stuck in their pasts. In time, a person may wish to consider coming to terms with the hereditary patterns that have been passed down through his or her genetic makeup. Our DNA, our "genes," hold the memories of past generations. Even for those readers who have a belief system that includes the living of a past life, forgiveness has the power to supersede the suffering of our ancestors.

People may also choose to examine their cultural codes, which encompass language, ideas, beliefs, customs, institutions, tools, techniques, works of art, rituals, and ceremonies, among other elements. The means of forgiveness allows one to let loose the cultural codes that do not ring true for him or her, accepting the ones that do.

Forgiveness can help one explore the social beliefs of the day along with the pressures of behavior expected of an individual who occupies a given social position or status. A role, or a pattern of behavior that is socially recognized, provides the means of identifying and placing an individual in that society. A role, or a "label," identifies a social position, such as that of a corporate president or of a janitor in that same corporation. Within our own families, our placement, our role, can also serve as a strategy for coping with recurring situations and dealing with the roles of others, such as parent-child roles.

Our parents or our caretakers assigned each of us a role to play out in the family. We accepted this role as true and we carried this theme all through school and into our work and community. The question is: Is that role you were assigned as a child still functioning for you today? Discovering your main role and recognizing how it is being played out in your adult life can be an important avenue to explore. Whatever your role may be, it is not right or wrong; discovering it just gives you greater options to live by once you understand what it is.

Here are a few examples of roles you might have been assigned: People have been labeled the "pleaser personality," the "caretaker," or the "savior." For others it may have been the "favorite one," the "smart one," the "winner," the "responsible one." Does the position of the "loser," the "outlaw," the "outsider," or the "rebel" sound familiar? Were you the "strong, athletic type"? Or were you labeled the "accident-prone, clumsy one"? You may discover that you have been given several roles, yet you will notice one dominant position, one that stands out more than the others.

If you choose to practice the forgiveness process as instructed here, you will no longer cling to or wallow in your anger or pain, nor even hold onto your "roles" if you choose to let them go.

This procedure, which is explained in greater detail in the following chapters, is a tool that you can use in the privacy of your own home. It is solid, it is empowering, it is an emotional bridge that a person can use to move forward in his or her life. Letting go is good for everyone!

Beginning to Forgive

Pause and reflect. Again, take a few deep, relaxing breaths and ask yourself these questions to determine if you are ready to begin the forgiveness process.

- Are you accepting the past as being over?
- What is your circumstance costing you if you do not let go?

- When you are up against it and feeling cornered, blocked, or just plain stuck, where do you start?

- When life seemingly is not working in one or more areas, such as mental, physical, emotional, spiritual, or financial, what do you do?

- Are you ready to let go of what appears not to be working?

Forgiveness is a bold choice. To forgive is the key to freeing yourself from any person, place, thing, or situation that no longer serves you in a positive way. Choosing to forgive gives relief from past pain and opens up the possibility for greater joy, peace, and security in daily life.

CHAPTER TWO SUMMARY

- Forgiveness is a key to letting go of emotional blocks and bondage, thus freeing ourselves for positive opportunities in all areas.

- Making a bold decision to forgive and let go empowers us to break free from hereditary patterns, cultural codes, and social beliefs that no longer serve us.

- By forgiving, we take responsibility for our attitudes.

"Whoever may torment you, harass you, confound you, or upset you, is a teacher. Not because they're wise, but because you seek to become so."

—Anonymous

A Mother's Passing and a Daughter's Story of Forgiveness

By Phyllis

In sitting with my mother as she made her journey between life and death, I had many hours and days to dwell on our relationship, our "dance." It had never been an easy one: me, sensitive, longing for a loving mother; her, insensitive, always wanting me to be more, do more, be best in everything, but always judged as just a little lacking.

In my early forties I finally decided to just get over it, that it was just the way it was, and . . . to forgive her. This worked well for twenty-five years and now here we were, our last days together. I sang to her—she had given me the gift of music, working to buy me a piano and paying for my lessons. I read to her—she had read to us and encouraged a love of reading. And I told her I loved her and forgave her again and again. I wanted her to pass on feeling loved and forgiven.

The days stretched on and as I held her hands one morning, I realized that I had not always been kind in my thoughts and criticisms of her and perhaps I had not loved her as much as I could have. I thought about all this for awhile and realized that it would feel right to ask for her forgiveness. I did that. I asked that she forgive me for wanting more love from her than she could give or for wanting more kindnesses, which was not her nature. Although she was in her last state of stillness, I seemed to feel a change in her and, of course, in me. The hospice nurse suggested that we leave the window open that night as her soul might be leaving. And, at 2 a.m., it did. How grateful I was to have had the opportunity to explore both sides of forgiveness. We both could let go and just experience love.

CHAPTER 3

THE FORGIVENESS AFFIRMATION PROCESS

"Our intention creates our reality."
—Dr. Wayne W. Dyer

The Evolution of the Forgiveness Process

The act of forgiving is one of our most misunderstood concepts. I admit that my own knowledge about and understanding of the subject of forgiving was minuscule to none. I wondered whether the act of forgiving was something that came naturally, or was it an acquired skill that needed to be learned? I became highly motivated to investigate further (my story appears at the conclusion of this chapter).

After I personally experienced the benefits of writing forgiveness affirmations, I pondered whether others could duplicate this simple writing process with equal or better results. As opportunities arose, I would share with others the stories about the successes in my life that came through writing forgiveness affirmations and they too became interested in the process. They in turn would tell me of challenging situations in their own lives and wonder if this forgiveness writing I described would also work for them.

After explaining how I had written forgiveness affirmations, I encouraged them to begin writing on their personal challenges. They began to copy what I had done and started seeing changes in their own lives almost immediately.

As these people learned how the process worked, which I explain later in this chapter, they encountered several types of obstacles. For example, in some cases, people were not always sure they wanted to give up their resentment and anger. They saw it as a sign of weakness. Some thought they would be giving approval to an act that had hurt them deeply. Others felt justified in not forgiving the situation at all.

Breaking the Cycle

Researching further, I learned that carrying around suppressed emotions such as anger, guilt, fear, resentment, and bitterness *can destroy our lives*. Science has found evidence that the refusal to release and let go of past injuries can have a physiological impact on us by creating addictions, divisions, and unsatisfying relationships. Illness and disease are also possible.

Without truly letting go through forgiveness, we may find ourselves "stuck" by living the pain over and over again in various forms. We will keep living it and revictimizing ourselves as long as we hold an attachment to the past! Forgiveness is a means by which to break this cycle.

The Power of Writing

One well-known and constructive method to "let off steam" is to write down on paper any upsetting emotion; we can tear up the paper later. Through this expressive, therapeutic style, we are releasing our anger in a harmless, safe, and appropriate way.

An article from the *Sydney Morning Herald* (November 10, 2005)[1] describes how patients have used writing as a therapeutic tool and have seen it lead to profound transformations in their health.

> A growing body of research concludes that "writing from the heart" literally heals your heart, blood pressure and other stress-related diseases....

> One study that tested expressive writing's impact on the immune system found patients improved significantly. After only three writing sessions lasting 20 minutes on consecutive days, months later people

suffering asthma recorded better lung function, and those with rheumatoid arthritis had less inflammation and pain. (p. 6)

The article, which describes a clinical psychologist's work on expressive writing, goes on to say:

Evidence suggests that writing helps organise the memories into a story, and encourages the mind to process events. "It helps connect people to their emotions, moves them forward over time, and then helps them change the way they think about it," [Dr. Karen] Baikie says. (p. 6)

According to an article by Frankie D. Lemus, MA, in the Winter 2006 edition of *Paradigm*:[2]

Interactive Journaling® is an experiential writing process that guides and motivates people toward positive lifestyle change. It is the vehicle by which best practices in a variety of modalities (e.g., cognitive-behavioral, 12-Step) can be applied in a format that serves the individual as a personalized tool for change. (p. 8)

Lemus, citing Adams, says the study of the power of writing dates back as far as the 1950s:

> Ira Progoff...began experimenting with the style and method of journal writing in his clinical practice in 1957. Progoff was a Jungian-trained psychotherapist who refined the model of holistic depth psychology in written self-expression.... Progoff began implementing a "psychological workbook" with his clients as an adjunct to psychotherapy. He asked people to keep a notebook, or journal, to record events of their inner life....He documented a specific process that could be evoked more actively by the use of a journal procedure. (p. 8)

The article goes on to say:

> Kathleen Adams is the founder of The Center for Journal Therapy, and has been conducting workshops on journaling and teaching its therapeutic uses since 1985. She emphasizes journaling's application as a tool for personal growth and self-discovery for individuals who want to learn how to "heal" themselves; and even suggests that

journaling is the marriage of writing and psychotherapy. (p. 9)

In the *Journal of Abnormal Psychology,* James W. Pennebaker and Sandra Klihr Beall write about a study they performed in the 1980s:[3]

> In recent years, evidence has accumulated indicating that not disclosing extremely personal and traumatic experiences to others over a long period of time may be related to disease processes. (p. 274)

They asked participants to write about feelings that were associated with a traumatic event in their lives for fifteen to twenty minutes a night for three to four consecutive nights. They found that those who wrote about these feelings, rather than more trivial things, showed significantly greater increases in health during the next four to six months. They conclude:

> As our study has indicated, one need not orally confide to another. Rather, the mere act of writing about an event and the emotions surrounding it is sufficient to

reduce the long-term work of inhibition. (p. 281)

As we can see, writing is an important "action." This action taken is what fuels results and what makes "writing" forgiveness so powerful. Let us begin the journey.

Taking Action

Action 1: Set Your Forgiveness Intentions

Setting forgiveness intentions greatly assists you in achieving results. Say out loud the following three sentences:

1. The facts are now revealed.
2. The actions necessary are now made known.
3. The circumstances will now improve.

After setting your intention, you are now ready to begin the forgiveness process through the act of writing forgiveness affirmations.

"Know thy self, and you will know the universe."
—Interpretation of an inscription in the Temple at Delphi, Greece

Action 2: Identifying Your Issue

To the best of your ability, identify any one or more people, places, things, or situations that are causing any stress or upset in your life right now. List *anything* that disturbs you when you think about it. Write down all your issues on a sheet of paper, in whatever order they come to mind. The following samples list some common subjects.

Samples of possible person(s):

Father	Yourself	Children
Mother	Relatives	Landlords
Caretaker	Partner	Friends
Siblings	Politicians	Neighbors
Employers	Employees	Customers
Roommates	Classmates	Teachers
Ex-Partners	Professionals	Abusers

Samples of possible place(s):

Workplace	School	Cities
Home	Institutions	Prison
Neighborhood	Courts	Countries
Banks	Hospitals	Government Offices

Samples of possible thing(s):

Feelings	Beliefs	Ideas
Disease	Terrorism	Environmental Issues
Attitude	Objects	Car
Credit Cards	Debts	Grades
Famine	Gossip	Health
Addictions	Technology	Habits
Limitations	Lack	Drama/Trauma

Samples of possible situation(s):

Marriage	Divorce	Births
Deaths	Lawsuits	Bankruptcy
Audit	Holidays	Bureaucracy
Interviews	Accidents	Disasters
War	Reunions	Homelessness

Complete your list of issue(s). From this list, select one that you would like to forgive and release right now.

"As I forgive, I begin anew."

—Daily Word

Action 3: Writing Forgiveness Affirmations

Webster's Dictionary defines the act of affirming as: "To make firm; to assert positively; to tell with confidence; declare; allege; opposed to deny; to confirm or ratify; to make a solemn assertion or declaration; to make a legal affirmation."

Through the act of affirming something, you make it more effective. Therefore, a forgiveness affirmation is the solemn assertion and declaration of forgiving something and the affirmation of that act of forgiving as being true.

You can take the affirmation process to a higher level of effectiveness by writing it down. By applying the power of a written affirmation in your unique situation, you can begin your forgiveness process.

Taking pen and paper in hand, write your first forgiveness affirmation. Write the words "I forgive," followed by whatever you identified in Action 2 as being the issue that you have chosen to forgive and release.

Writing forgiveness affirmations is as easy as this!

Examples of writing affirmations:

- Writing forgiveness on any *person:*
  I forgive <u>my partner </u>(write partner's name)

- Writing forgiveness on any *place:*
  I forgive <u>my work</u> (write company's name)
- Writing forgiveness on any *thing:*
  I forgive <u>prejudice</u>.
- Writing forgiveness on any *situation:*
  I forgive <u>political corruption</u>.

Through this writing process you will experience a sense of relief and peace of mind regarding your issue. There is something magical and miraculous about the action of writing forgiveness affirmations.

For some, writing just one forgiveness affirmation will bring the peace of mind they seek. It may take others an entire page or more to bring the relief and peace of mind they desire. This is why this process is unique. It is automatically customized according to each individual's needs. The amount of writing isn't important; the fact that you are writing on your issue is. *The power is in the action of writing!*

As you begin to write your affirmation(s) on your original issue, it is not uncommon that another person, place, thing, or situation pops into your mind, apparently out of nowhere. This is a natural occurrence. What to do? I suggest writing on whatever comes to mind at that moment. The flow of thoughts that pop up needs to be acknowledged. The main idea is to write until you feel better. You are writing for peace of mind and relief. The acknowledgment of the random thoughts that come to you help you achieve this. To help you understand how this process works, I will give you an example of a relationship issue on which I wrote.

How the process works—A real-life example:

My intention, at the time, was to bring out the facts of the underlying cause of stress between my partner and me. I desired a solution to the problem and that our circumstances would improve. I chose to write forgiveness on my partner and began by writing forgiveness affirmations as follows:

I forgive my partner
I forgive my partner
I forgive my partner

While I was writing the words *I forgive my partner*, the word *control* popped into my mind. I began to write forgiveness on this new word, *control.*

I forgive control
I forgive control
I forgive control

I wrote on this new word as many times as I needed. I continued to write until I either felt better or something else entered my mind.

While writing on the word *control,* I also wrote down any further random phrases that were connected to the word. I then wrote:

I forgive control
I forgive the control
I forgive feeling out of control

While I was writing on the phrases and variations surrounding the word *control,* the word *pressure* popped into my mind. I began to write forgiveness on the word *pressure* just as I had with the previous word *control.* I then wrote:

I forgive the pressure
I forgive the pressure I feel

While I was writing the words *I forgive the pressure,* the word *fear* popped into my mind. I felt it necessary to write only one affirmation on the word *fear*. I then wrote:

I forgive fear

After I wrote *I forgive fear* once, the word *myself* sprang to mind. I then wrote forgiveness affirmations on the word *myself*. I wrote:

I forgive myself
I forgive myself
I forgive Sunnee

As I wrote the phrase *I forgive Sunnee*, a sense of peace came over me. I knew at this point that I was done and that the process had come full circle. I knew I was complete because I was more mentally and physically relaxed about the situation than I was before I started.

Writing uncovers the facts

The conclusion of the writing can be different for some people, but in most cases people feel a lessening of the stress associated with the issue they are writing on. The intensity of the upset surrounding the original issue decreases.

The result of my writing example was a greater peace of mind, and through this state of greater serenity came the intuitive awareness that my partner and I needed a deeper level of honest and open communication. This was the true, underlying, unseen truth causing the upset that was the original motivation for writing *I forgive my partner*. All this came about through the power of my writing simple forgiveness affirmations, and it took less than five minutes.

The writing revealed the facts surrounding my situation. I allowed the truth to surface and through my newfound awareness I was able to take actions toward a positive resolution between my partner and me. Those "actions" are revealed or made known generally by intuition, that gut feeling. That "inner feeling," that "inner voice" within you, is where you will place the most energy and time. It is in the follow-through that successful change will manifest itself.

In conclusion, all you need to do is to start with one subject and write on whatever else comes to your mind. Let your random thoughts be your guide to your writing. This process leads you along through your own conscious and unconscious thinking patterns. This is why this process is unique; it is customized and personalized just for you.

What's important here is to just allow the thoughts to flow and continue to write until you have a sense of relief and peace of mind. This sense of well-being is the indicator that you have completed writing for the moment.

Two people can write on the same subject matter, using the same affirmations, and still receive different results. Since we are all distinctive individuals, no two people or their states of affairs are alike, even though they may appear similar.

Action 4: Repeat Writing If You Feel the Need

Repeat writing as often as necessary until you have achieved peace of mind. If at any time your issue resurfaces and triggers an upset in you, begin writing on that issue again. Keep writing until you feel calmer. Continue with your forgiveness writing affirmations until any or all of the following happens:

1. The facts are revealed.
2. The actions necessary are made known.
3. The circumstances improve.

CHAPTER THREE SUMMARY

- There is significant evidence to suggest that writing/journaling in general is a powerful tool for permanent and positive lifestyle change.

- Writing forgiveness affirmations is the "action" that fuels results and what makes "writing" forgiveness so powerful.

- Forgiveness Affirmation Writing Steps:

  Action 1: Set yourself up for success—set your intentions before writing.

  Action 2: Identify the obvious upset(s).

  Action 3: Write forgiveness affirmations on your upset or challenging issue.

  Action 4: Repeat writing if you feel the need to restore peace of mind.

"All that we are is the result of what we have thought."

—Buddha

"Judgment is the projection of one's own stuff on another. Forgiveness is letting that stuff go."

The Author's Forgiveness Story

Through this unique process of forgiveness writing, I am now able to tell my story without guilt, blame, or shame. My intention is to inspire and empower all who read this story and the numerous stories throughout the book, all generously shared by others who have also used this process. My hope is that readers will draw the courage from within themselves to use this forgiveness process to instill positive changes in their own lives.

Within one week of writing my first forgiveness affirmations, I discovered that the man who raised me and who I had thought was my biological father my entire life was not my father after all.

About twenty-five years ago, I experienced what I call a "wake-up call" that opened my awareness to a greater spiritual awakening. At that time, I was separated from my husband, with all the indicators flashing before my eyes that the two of us were traveling down the road toward a divorce.

My emotional state was at an all-time low. One evening, feeling great despair, I looked upward toward the ceiling of my kitchen and screamed at

God: "I need help and I need it now!" In moments I heard a very quiet voice whisper, "Forgive your father."

I yelled back, "I have nothing to forgive my father for!" I heard the quiet voice repeat the words, "Forgive your father." This conversation continued in my kitchen for a few minutes—with my responding out loud each time. Remember, reader, no one was in that kitchen but me. Looking back, I see how strange it must have seemed and how ridiculous I must have looked, standing alone in the kitchen talking toward my ceiling. Yet this voice was very real.

Days went by. I could not shake those words loose from my thoughts. Forgive? What did that mean? How did I go about doing it? I honestly did not know how to begin, what to do.

I was brought up in a Christian belief system. All I could recollect regarding forgiveness were the words that Jesus Christ spoke when in agony at the time of his death. "Forgive them, for they know not what they do."

I again found myself standing in the middle of my kitchen on a Saturday evening, reflecting on the words I heard a month before: "Forgive your father." I immediately became inspired to write something down. I proceeded to take one of my children's school notebook papers and write the numbers 1 through 100 on a sheet of lined paper. After each number I wrote these words, "I forgive you Dad." This one sentence, "I forgive you Dad," was repeated 100 times. Or so I thought. . . .

On Sunday morning, I decided to review the forgiveness phrases I had written the night before. I quickly glanced at the written list, thinking to evaluate it because I had an interest in handwriting analysis, when the very first sentence drew my eyes. To my alarm, instead of "I forgive you Dad," the first sentence that I had written read, "I hate you Dad." Chills went up and down my spine! I froze when I read that phrase. I honestly did not remember writing those words. I recall saying to myself that I did not want to hate anyone. Yet, I could not deny what I had written and I never remembered doing it!

I was so shocked by what I obviously had written and by the possibility that I might have a deep-seated, unconscious issue with my father. Again and again I asked myself, "What could it possibly be?" I was curious to know if any additional information would surface if I continued to write that same sentence, "I forgive you Dad." Hence, that evening I again wrote "I forgive you Dad" 100 times.

I felt as if I were a guinea pig undergoing experiments in a laboratory, and here I had volunteered for it without knowing the outcome. For seven days total, I would sit in my kitchen in the quiet of the evening and write "I forgive you Dad" 100 times.

On the eighth day, a Monday morning, something totally unexpected happened. After placing my children on their school bus, I intended to go about my normal day. I proceeded upstairs to my bedroom to make my bed and suddenly, out of nowhere, I found myself on the floor in a fetal position, rocking and crying. It happened that fast! I continued rocking and crying in that fetal position for the entire day, up until an hour before my children returned home from school. This feeling "lifted and cleared" as fast as it had come over me. I could not understand what had happened, yet I felt better than I had felt at any time in my entire life. I was so excited and jazzed at this newfound feeling of bliss. I thought back to the fact that the only thing that I had done differently during the past week was to write forgiveness affirmations on my father. What did this mean?

I was puzzled by what had happened, although it appeared to me that through my handwriting I had tapped into some deep-seated emotion that

I had masked for most of my life. It also became obvious to me that there was a connection between my writing and what I was feeling. No words could describe my elation that I had finally found something that worked and that was so simple to carry out.

I had journaled for only a week and it became apparent that somehow during this experience I had gotten back in touch with my feelings and that my feelings were dictating what I should do next. This intuitive, gut feeling was urging me to phone my mother and inform her I was coming home for a visit. I was hesitant to return home since my mother and I did not have a very close relationship.

The Christian denomination that I was brought up in had ostracized me from the congregation. I was considered a "lost soul." Those who still practiced this religion were not to talk to me or associate with me—this included my entire family. Even under those circumstances and knowing that my visit would be quite awkward and strained, I held my position and made arrangements to visit my mother.

After I arrived, I expressed openly to my mother my feelings that I didn't feel I was a part of our family. I told her that I felt as if I were adopted, and that I didn't understand why I had those feelings.

My mother had her back to me, yet after I expressed my thoughts, she immediately wheeled around, looked directly at me, and said, "You are right! The father that you thought was your father is not your biological father. In fact, I had an affair, and you're the child born from that affair." My mother continued, "I was always afraid to tell you in fear that you would be mad at me." Hearing those words of my mother's was a massive validation and a freeing experience that no words could possibly express. I was so thrilled to hear this truth from her that I literally picked her up, swirled her around, and screamed, "I'm not crazy after all!" At that moment, her words confirmed the numerous feelings that I had had as a child of not fitting in as part of our family. All those years I had felt so crazy, and maybe, through this courageous disclosure on my mother's part, I was just beginning to understand what being "intuitive" meant. This experience was the beginning of giving myself permission to trust my own feelings instead of second-guessing myself. It was time to wake up and come out alive. Thank you, mother!

Just as a rock thrown into a pond creates a ripple effect in water, my experience of writing forgiveness affirmations continues to make profound changes occur in my life and in those of countless others. I consider this to be no less than a miracle, a breakthrough into the unconscious mind, which is 95 percent to 96 percent of our thoughts, according to researchers. An article in *American Demographics* (March 1, 2003) quotes consumer marketing research guru Gerald Zaltman of Harvard University, who says:

> Consumers can't really describe their decision-making process because they "have far less access to their mental activities than marketers give them credit for—95 percent of thinking takes place in the unconscious mind."[4]

I recall that even as a six-year-old child, I would hear that voice speak to me when I was in my backyard, saying, "You will remember the truth."

That "truth," as I understand it, is a "universal forgiveness truth." It crosses all boundaries of nationality, political affiliation, economic status, social position, age, educational level, or religious faith. This "truth" is free and available to all who choose to use it.

After nearly a quarter of a century of writing forgiveness affirmations, I have concluded that for anyone and everyone who will write forgiveness, at least these three benefits, or more, will occur:

1. The facts are revealed.
2. The actions necessary will be made known.
3. The circumstances will improve.

I consider the forgiveness writing process as my "lifeline" in dealing with any challenges I may have. As long as I have a mind and body, I will continue to write forgiveness affirmations for greater peace, freedom, and joy in my life.

My intent as I disclose my story is to inspire and challenge you, the reader, to improve the quality of your own life no matter how small or great. Seek the hidden treasures awaiting you in this world through the power of forgiveness.

CHAPTER 4

THE SIX PHASES OF FORGIVENESS

This chapter will help you to identify which emotional phases you may experience during your personal forgiveness process. Understanding the phase you are in will help you monitor your progress in the forgiveness method.

It is important to understand that there are six basic phases of forgiveness. These six phases can occur in any order. They may occur at different levels of intensity for different lengths of time depending on the individual. There is no right or wrong order in which to move through these phases. At any one time or another in our lives, we can experience one or more of these phases, either consciously or unconsciously.

Identifying which phase we find ourselves experiencing is the first step in liberating ourselves to progress beyond it.

Identifying the Six Phases

Denial

In this stage, the person is not ready or is refusing to deal with the person, place, thing, or situation.

When a person does decide to come out of denial, and to see the situation for what it really is, he or she is half the way there to shifting or improving his or her circumstances.

Self-Blame

This is the phase of regretting, a negative self-talk that says, "I could have made it better or maybe it wouldn't have happened if only I *could* have, *should* have, or *would* have done something differently." This internal voice creates barriers.

Victimhood

This phase is one in which the person has a lack of healthy personal boundaries and a tendency to be "needy" or codependent. Emotional feelings might include helplessness, hopelessness, a sense of being trapped, feeling "used" by others, and martyrdom. In this stage, we have feelings of low self-esteem, which is a function of how we perceive others' viewing us. Victimhood can show up in a person's being a "pleaser" and a "giver" type at his or her own expense, which can bring about passive-aggressive behavior. The bottom line is that victims do not believe they are "enough."

Anger

The situation may trigger anger about and/or resentment of life's unfulfilled expectations. A deeper level of anger may surface as rage. Underlying the emotion of anger is the emotion of fear. The goal is to find an avenue to express the anger in a positive and constructive manner and to no longer suppress it. Writing forgiveness affirmations is extremely beneficial in recognizing and releasing anger.

Survival

These people have recognized that they have been hurt and now rise above it by deciding to experience something better. They take stock in themselves by becoming grateful, appreciating what they have in their lives now, and defining their needs and wants. They then set realistic goals, knowing they deserve to be happy, and take the necessary action to obtain them.

Full Integration—The New Person

At this level, people will rise above the situation and take responsibility for themselves and their life's affairs. They now claim their birthright to be happy and take the necessary steps to give themselves the best lives ever. With new attitudes, they focus on what they prefer to experience instead.

As we live in this final phase of integration, the ultimate goal is to integrate all five of the previous stages as follows:

1. **Recognizing denial:** In this stage you acknowledge your state of denial. You now choose to take responsibility for your own happiness. You have become sick and tired of being sick and tired. You realize where your energy flows is where your attention goes. With your new attitude, you are willing to make changes.

2. **Surrendering self-blame:** You are no longer blaming yourself and others. You have reached a level of acceptance that everyone concerned was doing the best he or she could do at the time. Through time, compassion sets in the heart. You start to understand, feel, and recognize how the others involved were possibly living in fear or taking another path. This is where the tool of writing forgiveness offers the opportunity to release and let go of the emotional attachment to a situation.

3. **Letting go of victimhood:** You have now risen above living as a victim and a martyr by establishing healthier boundaries for yourself. You have moved beyond the phase of "I can't." You also have a new attitude, realizing that life is not the way it's supposed to be; it is the way it is. It is the way you cope that makes all the difference in your situation. This is the phase in which you take back your personal power through a newfound sense of desirability. Having reached a higher plane of self-esteem and self-worth, you now have the ability to: *Ask, believe* you deserve it, *receive* with an attitude of gratitude, and *visualize* as if you already have it.

4. **Releasing anger:** You have let go of the anger and other negative emotions attached to the circumstances. You now perceive your situation as an opportunity to move past the anger by creating constructive and healthy outlets and developing communication skills.

5. **Integrating survival:** You have accepted that you have been hurt.

You now decide to learn from the experience and move beyond it. You understand that nothing new can come into your life unless you are grateful. You feel appreciation for and are now able to express gratitude for your experience. Quite possibly, you can say or write with meaning: "I forgive and love you," as you have come to a space where you recognize the gift in the situation.

Moving Through the Six Phases

It is important to understand that the forgiveness process will be a personal journey through these six phases. By being honest with ourselves, we can understand which phase we are experiencing at the moment. The objective is not to get stuck or become immovable but to grow personally and live in the final integration stage.

A key element of forgiveness as we travel through these phases is not having an attachment to the final outcome. Allowing the truth surrounding a situation to surface, no matter what that truth may be, takes great courage. Be prepared to accept whatever happens as being the highest and best good for all concerned.

Understand that there is no right or wrong timeline for "being" in any one of these phases.

I encourage individuals to be patient, gentle, and kind with themselves during their process.

Allow the path of forgiveness to bring you to a place of surrender, and in that very second of surrender, there is peace.

CHAPTER FOUR SUMMARY

- An individual will experience one or more of the basic six phases of the forgiveness process.

- Identifying which phase you are experiencing enables you to free yourself and move beyond it.

- There is no right or wrong order in which to move through these phases.

- Each individual can experience these six phases or stages in any order, any level of intensity, or any length of time.

- Most important, be patient; be gentle and kind with yourself.

- Surrendering control over the final outcome is what sets us free. In that very moment, you will experience peace of mind.

"I let go of resentment.
I let it be easy.

I give up the need to control.
With God as my ally, who can be against me?

Everyone is right—for where they are.
I release all judgments.

I see everyone as my teacher—what can I learn from this situation?
I release the past and live in the present.
I let the future take care of itself."

—Soul Esteem Center

The Neighbors from Hell
By Joan Laue

For two years, I felt trapped as a victim in my own home by a very dysfunctional family living next door to me. The family included a single mother and her three young daughters, ages ten, thirteen, and fifteen. The mother appeared to be absent much of the time, which allowed the older daughters to reign freely and turn our neighborhood upside down.

I lost my peaceful enjoyment of my home, as did my other neighbors, for a year. Imagine loud rock music blasting from open car doors both in front and in back of my home, kids parking to block my entry and smoking marijuana. The boom-box cars were so loud I could not share a cup of tea with a friend on my back deck. Since the girls' mother slept elsewhere many nights and was away working during the day, there appeared to be no parental supervision and endless chaos almost twenty-four hours of the day and night. The home from hell next door became a free boardinghouse for delinquent juvenile males, who partied all night and threw glass liquor bottles into the alley to shatter into piles of broken glass, which I swept up daily. These kids apparently did not go to school as they were around all day and night, yelling and getting into all the trouble they could.

These challenging teenagers ripped up all the political signs of the would-be mayor and others running for election in our town. They used these signs as if they were Frisbees in the street or on the lawns of homeowners. They destroyed the signs by jumping on them and they could not be replaced. The gang of approximately ten young juveniles with nothing better to do yelled, screamed, hung out on the streets, killed a neighbor's cat, cut off its genitals, and dumped it on my front porch steps. One male juvenile assaulted and battered my elderly neighbor across the street. The kid spent one night in juvenile hall and was released the next morning.

The fifteen-year-old daughter led groups of mostly boys out of the cellar door with supplies of drugs and used a neighbor's vacant barn to host drug parties. These endless activities kept the police busy, and I became extremely tense and stressed. There seemed to be no escape for me. I felt trapped and victimized in my own home.

One day Sunnee came to help me with the forgiveness process. First, I related all the grief, pain, the agony and the anger, the helplessness of feeling victimized. Sunnee wrote down every feeling that I purged and read the list back to me so I could fully acknowledge what I was experiencing. After she heard me completely, she asked, "Are you ready to let go of this huge emotional poison?"

We wrote forgiveness affirmations on all of the people and the situations that surrounded the circumstances. My final words were: "I now release and let go of this entire situation."

After identifying what I obviously did not want to experience any longer, I was able to focus on what I preferred to experience instead. I visualized a wonderful, friendly middle-aged couple moving into the house next door...this or something better! I prayed and the couple did come a few months later after the house was vacated next door.

The amazing miracle to me was that within three or four days of doing the forgiveness process with Sunnee, the whole nasty goings-on just stopped and the neighborhood was quiet. No yelling, no gangs taking over the neighborhood. The nightmare evaporated like *magic!* To this day I see the miracle of true heartfelt forgiveness, which is so powerful. It is as if you're hooked onto a bungee cord and you keep bouncing back to the same problem. Forgiveness helps you to unhook yourself from people you need to let go of.

CHAPTER 5

WHAT WOULD YOU PREFER INSTEAD?

Life is full of choices. Compare life to one giant smorgasbord. At this feast, you can choose from countless varieties of foods: vegetables, meat/ protein, fruits, and desserts. It's an abundance of choices! A few of life's smorgasbord choices that you will make might include such things as your education, career, relationships, children, residence, finances, and health. As we "taste" numerous life experiences, we learn and discover through time what we prefer to experience, what works for us, and what doesn't.

Thus far, we have learned a universal message, the powerful way to erase events that no longer serve our highest good. When we choose to surrender to this process of letting go, we will bring about a space in which we are now free to choose something different. Through the act of forgiving, we literally have begun the process to create with purpose; we have created a clean slate. When we do so, life affords us the opportunity to choose a different path.

In general, people want love, happiness, peace, joy, freedom, health, and wealth. Most often, what we prefer is just the opposite of the "power eraser" that we have released through forgiveness affirmation writing.

By practicing forgiveness, we automatically create a shift in our outlooks and transform our perceptions. We release our judgment. When something is neither good nor bad, we can shift into a neutral position, and in this space we become free—free to choose something different. Complete forgiveness requires the willingness to take a proactive step toward reclaiming our personal power. If a person has a belief that there is nothing that can be done to improve a situation, he or she produces an entrapped mind. Even a slight shift in conscious thought can be the key to unlocking the limitless possibilities that the smorgasbord of life has to offer. This is true personal power!

As explained earlier, writing forgiveness affirmations will shed light upon the truth. The facts will be revealed, the necessary actions will be made known, generally through an intuitive or "gut" feeling, and one can anticipate that the circumstances will improve.

A Change for the Positive

The question of what we truly desire can be a challenging topic for many people. Listen closely to people's conversations and you just may find that they will speak endlessly of situations they don't want. On and on they will talk and complain. This is an excellent opportunity to ask, "What do you prefer instead?" or "What do you desire now?" Here are a few ways to help you develop a shift to the positive.

Attitude of Gratitude

The first quality to bring forth from within us is an attitude of gratitude. Expressing thankfulness, appreciation, and gratefulness for what we already have in our lives gives us a springboard from which we can begin to attract something better. For example, you are invited to a dinner party and you tell the host how much you are enjoying the food that was prepared and served. The host will more than likely ask you if you would like a second helping; the host offers you more because *you were appreciating.* This is a universal law of attraction, and this law will always give you more of what you are grateful for. Anytime you appreciate what is in your life, you will open the door to attract more of it.

Focus on what you want more of in your life and it will expand. Talk about what you prefer to experience as if it were in your life right now! Give gratitude throughout the day. Look for reasons to be grateful. Nothing new can come into your life unless you are grateful. The famous and brilliant scientist, Albert Einstein, was known to say, "Thank you" 100 times, or more, each day.

We often take for granted the very things that most deserve our gratitude. Keeping a daily notebook or "gratitude journal" helps us recall areas in our lives that we may have once taken for granted; focusing on the good that has and is manifesting for us each day is empowering. Using the words "I am so grateful and happy that" or sentences beginning with "I love that," fill in the blank with sentences describing your deepest feelings of enthusiastic appreciation! Again, this is the universal law of attraction: What we focus upon, we attract more of. What we focus on, expands.

How to Determine What You Prefer Through Contrast

The second way to shift to the positive is to *ask*. The question now becomes "What would give me a greater sense of love, harmony, joy, freedom, health, and wealth?"

One method for discovering what you prefer is to use the power of contrast. This methodology involves identifying the upsetting traits of your situation by making a list for the sake of self-discovery. The next step is to identify what we desire by choosing the opposite of what we just listed. An example and directions of this method are as follows:

1. On a sheet of paper make two columns. In the left-hand column, make a list of the upsetting traits of your situation.

2. In the right-hand column, directly across from each upsetting trait, write down the positive traits that you would prefer to experience instead. Use the following illustration as a guide to create your own list.

Column 1	*Column 2*
My Forgiveness List of Any Person, Place, Thing, or Situation	*What I Prefer to Focus, Visualize, Attract, and Experience Instead*
(Write upsetting traits)	*(Write preferred traits)*
	I am now choosing to work with a supportive employer and I am so grateful.
Controlling boss	

Feeling victimized, restricted, and suppressed at work	I am declaring now that I have feelings of being valued and appreciated. I have flexible working conditions.
Low pay	I am proclaiming now to attract a better income with benefits and bonuses.
Gossiping and backstabbing coworkers	I am intending now to have attracted supportive, respectful, and honest coworkers.
Difficult commute	I am claiming now to have an enjoyable commute that's close to home and to love the process.

With this new awareness and now a new focus, we will begin to attract into our lives the people, the circumstances, and the events that will support this new creative desire. Using a negative person or situation as a "gift" of awareness, we can use "contrast" to distinguish between what is working and what is not.

We experience absolute sheer delight when we discover what brings joy into our lives. The joy, the enthusiasm that we exude, is contagious and will only multiply and manifest more of what we desire.

"If my new choice is right for me, bring it on!
If I am not making a choice for my highest good,
block it!"

—A Universal Thought for Manifesting
in Your Life

Releasing Attachment to the Final Outcome

Webster's definition of *attachment:*

> The act of attaching, any passion or liking which binds one person to another or to a place, etc.; that which attaches one object to another..."

On some level deep within us, we know that we need to make a change by letting go of negative thinking or way of being. When we decide to make this change, we may begin to separate ourselves from our comfort zone.

Many people are so fearful of the unknown that they would rather remain in their current situations than run the risk of change, even when their current situations do not serve them. At least their lives are familiar and they know what to expect.

When people decide to choose what they prefer to have, they can shift their lives for the better. Yet it is vital to release attachment to the final outcome in their situations.

What does this imply? We must refrain from being set on a particular outcome. We create only more anxiety when we try to control the outcome and to "make things happen." This is not to say that a person should not have hope for a certain outcome to occur. Yes, have a goal, some focused result. Yet be open for something *even better to occur*. Anyone thinking he or she can control or manipulate his or her situation with this forgiveness writing process will most likely *not* bring about a positive change. Instead, surrender to what you believe is your higher power, what you call or identify as your spirit source. Be still, be quiet, listen closely to your intuitive voice within for guidance, and follow through with the right action.

Forgiveness is the foundation for bringing about positive changes in your life. Yet if you hold a rigid grip on how you feel these changes should manifest themselves, you may cancel out the highest and best possible results. It is simply too exhausting to live in constant resistance, worry, fear, and distress over a particular end result.

The idea is to release control of your attachment to the final outcome. The forgiveness affirmation process helps you to have an honest assessment of the situation. This is a golden opportunity if you choose to shift cycles and patterns that are repeating in your life.

"The perfect people and
The ideal circumstances
and events are
Manifesting in my life now,
In just the perfect time,
Regardless of conditions,
In ways that totally delight me,
Beyond my expectations
For the benefit of all
Existence everywhere."

—A Universal Thought for Manifesting
in Your Life

CHAPTER FIVE SUMMARY

* Nothing new comes into your life unless you are grateful.

- Keeping a "gratitude journal" and writing what we appreciate and love in our lives right now allows us to receive more of it.

- It is OK to notice what you do *not* want. This is the gift of contrast, which aids us in discovering what we prefer to experience. Generally it is the opposite of what a person forgives and releases in his or her life.

- Once you discover what you prefer, focus only on that. Write it down, visualize it. Give thanks as if you already have it.

- Release attachment to the final outcome. Letting go of control for a certain outcome allows the good to manifest itself, quite possibly in better ways than you imagined.

"Forgiveness is almost a selfish act because of its immense benefits to the one who forgives."
—Lawana Blackwell
The Dowry of Miss Lydia Clark, 1999

"The only people with whom you should try to get even are those who have helped you."
—John E. Southard

Retirement, Relationships, and a Health Forgiveness Story
By Mr. M.

At the age of seventy-two, I was living in a retirement center and had been sitting in a wheelchair and breathing from a respirator for the past five years when I was introduced to Sunnee. I made an appointment with her to work with me.

In the privacy of my room, Sunnee and I together reviewed some of my background, my personal history. What appeared over and over again in the conversation was that I had a pattern of personal challenges with relationships. I desired more than anything to improve these relationships if there were a way. I begin writing forgiveness affirmations on three specific situations that were outlined for me, which were:

1. My adult daughter, now living in another state, who would not even speak to me and had accused me of sexual abuse.

2. The church that I was raised in, because of some possible underlying feelings of guilt and shame.

3. My first female role model, my mother.

In addition to writing forgiveness affirmations, I began taking a nutritional supplement that supports brain function so that it would help me in my assimilation and release of the underlying causes. Even though I had some skepticism, I rationalized that I had nothing to lose.

Exactly two weeks after my initial appointment with Sunnee, I was feeling rather mischievous and bought a pair of Rollerblades. I was raised on ice skates, yet I had never Rollerbladed before. I thought, "Why not?"

To stir up some excitement, I began Rollerblading inside and outside of the retirement center. However, I learned that stopping yourself on Rollerblades was different from stopping yourself on ice skates and I kept bumping into walls. The point is that I was out of the wheelchair and not breathing on my respirator 24/7 as I once was. I was actually having fun.

Relationships were shifting all around me. Remember my daughter who would not speak to me? She called me out of the blue within weeks of my writing and we had a conversation that at one time I thought would never occur. Then there were the nurses who worked at the retirement center; they began treating me differently. When they came into my room for regular nursing duties, they began showing me true affection. Even the other women living in the center were sensing that something was different about me.

To be honest, the changes occurred so quickly that I was a little overwhelmed by it all and yet it was exciting too.

CHAPTER 6

MASTERING OBSTACLES

Change is difficult. Anyone thinking that his or her situation remains apparently unchanged or that he or she is not moving forward during this writing process should not feel alone. Many people experience this apparent setback in the forgiveness process.

Addressing the Mind Chatter

The excuses, the fears, and/or resistances that can cross a person's mind become an internal dialogue known as mind chatter. This internal dialogue is trying to protect us and keep us feeling safe from being or continuing to be hurt. It is a human trait to experience this mind chatter. Some people refer to this mental conversation as monkey chatter, monkey mind, or self-mind talk. Actually, this chatter is our unconscious minds trying to rationalize why it is better and safer to stay where we are rather than to make a change. The closer we get to a real change or a breakthrough in our lives, the louder the internal chatter will become.

We come to a point at which we decide to either continue to live with our present circumstances or to experience something different. Most people will encounter this crossroad of choice. No matter how insignificant the situation may appear, this is the point at which a person must decide to walk past the mind chatter showing up in our lives as excuses, fears, and resistances. Recognizing and coming to terms with this internal mental dialogue takes perseverance, but it is what it means to be human. One solution when this internal mind chatter occurs is to recognize that it is happening. Give yourself a mental "thank you for sharing" and immediately refocus upon your objective of what you prefer to achieve.

If we are willing, we can use this opportunity to dig deeper within ourselves to ask the following important questions:

1. What excuses am I making about my situation?
2. What fears are surfacing in my mind?
3. What are my resistances to change?

This inquiry stirs a deliberate personal exploration, offering us the possible root causes of an obstruction to this process. This chapter is designed to create breakthroughs so the light of the genuine you can shine through.

The Excuses

Through the years people have expressed a variety of excuses for not writing forgiveness affirmations, such as:

"I don't have enough time." Writing one forgiveness affirmation takes approximately three to six seconds.

"I wrote once and it didn't work for me." Especially if a person has had a long-standing predicament or belief, then writing forgiveness affirmations on that particular problem may take more than one time. Being persistent in the writing will assist us in returning to a state of peace.

"I have so much to do already and it seems too simple to make a difference." A great teacher told me, "Truth is simple." Many times these excuses serve only to hold us back from our greater good. It is important to continue despite these doubts.

The Fears

Besides excuses, certain fears may arise surrounding the act of writing forgiveness. Fear of change and fear of the unknown have been the two most common obstacles people encounter.

People in general are creating the situations in their lives through these fears. People build emotional barriers to protect themselves from appearing weak or vulnerable. The fear of leaving our comfort zones or familiar situations is so challenging that we do not want to deal with it because ultimately we will have to take responsibility for how were creating the challenging situations in the first place. If people have not dealt with these fears of change and of the unknown, then all the forgiveness writing they do will have little impact on their situations. The reasons for these fears must be addressed on a core level, which usually means they are linked to whomever raised you as a child. This could apply to parents, stepparents, foster parents, family members (grandparents, aunts/uncles, half siblings), state institutions, day care, and so on.

Through my own fear I had built a symbolic wall for emotional protection; a fortress surrounded me. I made sure it was nice and thick. I would come out from behind this wall and "be" a certain way in public. Yet I always knew I could run behind my wall of protection and feel safe by hiding "the real me" from others. That was my protection, my shield from my own fears, until I discovered the forgiveness affirmation writing process. This process supported me while I identified several of the core issues that were the reasons behind my fears and it helped me change the destructive patterns in my life. The forgiveness helped me break my emotional connection with these fears and freed me to now create something that was more positive.

One day a friend inquired what this forgiveness process was doing for me. I told her about the symbolic, protective wall I had created. Except now, after writing for several months, I saw myself in front of that wall with my friends, and suddenly I realized I was naked and exposed in front of all of them. I quickly ran behind the wall to hide, only to notice that my wall was just one foot high. The forgiveness process had torn down the wall and I hadn't even noticed. There I was, with nowhere to hide, nowhere to go. Everyone could see me for who I was. As I spoke with my friend, I told her I was never going to go back, that I could never rebuild that wall.

Was fear knocking on my door? You bet. Instead of blaming others, I had to take responsibility for my life. I was afraid of what others might think, and I feared that I might lose status, that I might be alone, abandoned or rejected. I took personal responsibility by asking myself the following questions:

- Am I afraid of this forgiveness process's working?

- Am I afraid of confrontation?

- Am I afraid that if I change, will I disturb the status quo with family, friends, work?

- Am I making the wrong decision and am I going to regret it later?

- Am I going to create a "chain reaction" or a "domino effect" of events by doing something different?

These were some of the fears I faced as I asked myself if there were to be any changes in my life. I had to face my fears so I could set myself free. Without a doubt, the forgiveness affirmation writing process made it possible.

Fear can become a great emotional obstacle that keeps us from moving forward. Remember that holding onto that which does not serve us any longer will keep us blanketed in pain.

When writing forgiveness affirmations, an individual may experience the surfacing of emotional or physical symptoms. These emotions may have been lying dormant, yet they are already having an effect by immobilizing us, preventing us from moving forward or taking action in one or more areas of our lives. We use the act of writing forgiveness to nullify the "power eraser" and bring closure to these past traumas, which allows us to move through the sting of these related emotions. As we do this, we release their penetrating "hook" and in this transformation, the grip of our shadow side will diminish and fade.

The Resistances

In addition to excuses and fears, any number of resistances can also surface and hold one back from forgiving.

If you believe your affairs are unaffected by the writing process, it is important to look at the probable resistances. The following questions may help you discover the nature of these blocks.

Pause and reflect. Take a few deep, relaxing breaths and ask yourself these questions:

- Why am I resistant to the idea of forgiveness?
- What is my resistance to the forgiveness process's actually working?

- What is it that I think I am giving up; what do I think I am losing?

- What is my skepticism?

- What is my judgment or belief about forgiveness?

- What is behind my resistance to writing?

- Why do I want to hold on to a person, a place, a thing, or a situation that is no longer serving me in a positive way?

- Am I resistant to seeing my issue in a different way?

- What is my resistance to taking responsibility for my part in the situation?

What we resist will persist. Quite possibly, what we resist is change. Our personal search and development will help us to discover, acknowledge, and to come to terms with the underlying thoughts, feelings, and actions that may be blocking our highest good. Thus, it is important to look at the possible underlying causes if you believe your affairs are unaffected by this writing process.

1. How is my situation serving me? What am I learning from this?

2. What am I doing to contribute to my situation?

3. Do I think I have the right to be happy right now? Do I believe I am worthy to receive?

Thoughts, Feelings, Actions

For us to manifest the best life ever for ourselves, we must have three areas in alignment, which are our thoughts, our feelings, and our actions. If you are missing any one of these three, you will not get results.

Our thoughts create our feelings. Our feelings are the way the body communicates with us. By recognizing our feelings, we are literally connecting with our intuitive selves. We can tell if we are in alignment with our greater good by the way we feel. These feelings are not to be judged as good or bad. The feelings are the means for the body to tell us that something is in balance (joy) or out of balance (pain). We are either in harmony with or we are living out of harmony with our greater good. When we recognize this incredible gift, we can make the necessary adjustments to get ourselves back on track.

The next step is to align our thoughts and feelings with action. The action taken in this particular forgiveness process is manifested by the writing—not just thinking about it.

Let me illustrate how important it is to take the action to write and not just think about it. What makes legal documents, legal contracts, and legal agreements binding by law? It takes a handwritten signature of the parties involved to solidify the agreement. Notice that these parties do not print their names nor do they type their names—*they sign their names in writing.* Their written signature is a representation of who they are.

On some level, whether it is consciously or unconsciously made, when we write forgiveness affirmations we are signing a contract with ourselves to be open to shift our lives for the better. That is the truth. When we as humans align ourselves with truth, only good can come from this commitment.

Enlist Support

Human beings are relationship-making creatures. We function better within a supportive relationship environment or community. Depending on the individual's circumstances, it may be wise to enlist added support from others as an aid in the journey through this process. It has been found to be helpful for some to have one or more compassionate listeners available to assist in processing their emotions. Support can come from a trusted friend, a spiritual or religious representative, a counselor, a therapist, a life coach, or a group curriculum such as a twelve-step program that understands this writing process.

I recommend that your listeners be comfortable working directly with the feelings and emotions that may surface. They should be nonjudgmental, nonmanipulating, and noncontrolling. You ought to feel at ease in their presence. They should be warm and accepting and have a working knowledge of the forgiveness process. As you go through the process together, your listener or listeners should not pressure you to let go of any issue before you are capable or ready.

If it resonates with your beliefs, be willing to ask for divine assistance from what you believe to be your spiritual "Higher Power."

These are only suggestions that may help ease your self-discovery. Following what feels right and true for you is always encouraged.

Personal Discovery

Is it a wonder we have a tough time of it since so many intimate relationships fail?[5] After all, we learn how to create relationships from our parents and other adults around us, including older siblings. This is not to direct blame or point fingers toward them; maybe no one taught them either.

We will carry this pervasive parental/family legacy throughout our lives and into our relationships. The tendency is to gravitate to and attract the people, places, and circumstances—such as a marriage partner or a significant other—to aid us in our inner healing work.

Women generally, although not always, choose partners who remind them of their fathers or are the opposite of their fathers. Men have a general tendency to marry women who remind them of their mothers. Naturally, there can and will be exceptions.

For example, a client was having an extremely difficult time in her relationship with her husband. As she wrote forgiveness affirmations, she realized that the elements of his behavior that annoyed her so immensely were identical to her mother's irritating traits. By attracting her partner into her life, she was, in part, helping herself heal her inner mother wounds.

Yet, and quite often, relationships bring heartache. What to do? To be aware and understand the correlation between the partners we choose and/or our parents, we need to look at how we perceived our parents as our caregivers. Did you feel they were available to you mentally? physically? emotionally? financially? and/or spiritually? If your answer is yes, then congratulations! If not, and you felt one or more of these areas was neglected by one or both parent/guardians, then quite possibly that same area is going to present itself for the opportunity to heal in your adult life.

No matter what lifestyle we lead, we will attract to us the people, the events, and circumstances to mend the areas of our lives that need completion. This also applies to those who have been adopted or have lived in foster care and have never experienced being raised by a blood-family member.

Just observe those who have the tendency to "get under your skin." Let's say one of these is your employer. This employer, an authority figure, has the ability to push all your emotional buttons. Are those irritations, those annoying habits, or whatever they may be, familiar characteristics that you could trace back to a significant, influential adult from your past? Could you say the most irritating aspect of your boss reminds you of a parent, a guardian, a caretaker, a sibling? If so, forgiveness will set you free by mending your relationship with the present person and by healing the relationship with the person from the past, the beginning source. The objective of this personal discovery is to examine if there is a repetitive negative pattern beginning from infancy and continuing to adulthood so that we can release it, not attract more of it.

A pattern may demonstrate itself to us, let's say, in the form of repetitive rejection or abandonment in relationships. Or if our core safety and security issues need mending, we can expect them to surface for healing through life events. The main theme underscoring the wounded self for so many is that we are "just not enough." Yet, once they are identified, we have the options to break free of the wounds and construct another way of being.

I have created two charts: One outlines the masculine principles and one outlines the feminine principles. Within each of us we carry both qualities, the feminine and masculine behaviors. Think of these principles as like a battery with a positive and negative charge. For the battery to function, it must have both charges working in unison. The traditional male and female principles are to be used as a platform from which to launch into creating a richer and more fulfilling life.

If you are having challenges with money, which falls under masculine principles, I suggest beginning the forgiveness affirmation writing process with your first male role model. I highly recommend that women begin with the masculine principle, their father.

"I forgive my father"

Masculine Principles

- Money
- Power
- Authority
- Logical thought
- Focused action
- Manifestation into form
- Protection, strength, discipline

Writing forgiveness affirmations on the father can easily overflow into other areas that are generally associated in the world as masculine-dominated areas. The masculine manifests into reality in which the thought is that "more is better." The objective of the masculine is to have an intention, to aim toward, to reach goals. The masculine principle will acquire facts, analyze, and take action. Subjects such as mathematics, language, and scientific skills are considered masculine principles. Other areas falling under masculine principles are institutions such as banks, schools, universities, colleges, jails, prisons, weapons, war, autos (horse*power*), boats, planes, tanks, corporations, IRS/taxes, governments, police, armed services, presidents, CEOs, financial loans, bankruptcy, credit cards, debts, bills, professors, and teachers. The masculine also includes God the Father, religion, religious representatives, male family members such as grandfathers, stepfathers, male siblings, uncles, male partners, male friends. It is suggested that those with an eating disorder known as bulimia nervosa would do well to address the masculine areas with forgiveness.

"Your father may have given too little or too much. He may have been absent or overbearing, or perhaps a little of both. Whatever he has been, you must come to accept him and see what you have become in your emulation of him or your reaction to him. You must learn to understand him and forgive him. And you must learn to understand and forgive yourself. To know the divine Father, you must come to terms with the human one."
—Heartways Press, "Facing Our Father Wound" (Wisdom message for the week of June 19, 2007)

If you are having challenges with relationships, which fall under the feminine principle, then I highly recommend beginning your forgiveness writing with your first female role model. Generally, I suggest men begin their forgiveness affirmation writing process with the feminine principles, their mothers.

"I forgive my mother"

Feminine Principles

- Relationships, love/sexual power, intimacy/family/friendships, and social connections/community
- Communication/articulation
- Passivity, innate strength, mystery
- Intuition/self-knowledge/spirit
- Emotions/vulnerability
- Creativity in writing, art, music, dance
- Nurturer/anything regarding the mouth: food, diets (weight, shape), thumb sucking, nail biting, cigarettes

Writing forgiveness affirmations on the feminine principle is all about the power of relationships with everybody and everything. There is no place to go to be out of a relationship. It is about the interconnectedness, belonging, and about the interdependent world. This is an area that gives birth to children and ideas. Female areas will include our mother/mom, grandmothers, stepmothers, female siblings, female friends, and female partners as well as the Goddess aspects, divas, and Mother Earth. Included in this arena are intuitive healing, magnetic attraction, values, and qualities in an individual's world. Those with the eating disorder anorexia nervosa would do well to forgive in the area of the feminine principles.

If you are having a difficult time in relationships, whether it is a personal, social, or business relationship, look to see if the person has characteristics similar to those of a parent or influential adult from early childhood. This could include a sibling. Write forgiveness affirmations on the combination of people.

Dr. Harville Hendrix underscores these points in his book, *Getting the Love You Want: A Guide for Couples:*[6]

> We cover our wounds with healing ointment and gauze in an attempt to heal ourselves, but despite our efforts an emptiness wells up inside of us. We try to fill this emptiness

with food and drugs and activities, but what we yearn for is our original wholeness, our full range of emotions, the inquisitive mind that was our birthright, and the Buddha-like joy that we experienced as very young children. This becomes a spiritual yearning for completion, and, as in Plato's myth, we develop the profound conviction that finding the right person—that perfect mate—will complete us and make us whole. This special person can't be just anyone. It can't be the first man or woman that comes along with an appealing smile or a warm disposition. It has to be someone who stirs within us a deep sense of recognition: "This is the one I've been looking for! This is the one who will make up for the wounds of the past!"

And for reasons we will explore in greater depth...this person is invariably someone who has both the positive and the negative traits of our parents! (pp. 33–34)

Living in the Void

The "void," or as some may describe it, the "zone," is the time between the release of the old way and a rebirth or manifestation of a new way.

Every time we go through a change in our lives we will go through a void (or zone.) The duration of the void is determined by the emotional and psychological attachment we have to the old and familiar way. Experiencing the void is the purpose of writing forgiveness affirmations. We want to release the old to make way for the new.

A myriad of emotions can surface just being in the void. We may grieve the loss of the old, the familiar, and have apprehension or fear of the new, the unknown. Moving through the variety of emotions is why many people hesitate to move forward in this forgiveness process. They realize they must stretch beyond their comfort zone and move from the familiar to the unfamiliar.

During this period of the void you may feel a sense of loss or separation, yet this stage can also be the greatest opportunity. Since we have free will and choice, we can use this period to identify what we prefer to experience instead.

Let's Put the Excuses, the Fears, and the Resistances on the Table

It takes courage to face the excuses, fears, and resistances and this is why forgiving is the stuff of heroes.

Facing these internal feelings can be a huge hurdle in our ability to forgive. Taking responsibility for how we are feeling is one of the best ways we have of allowing ourselves to move forward in our lives. The more we are able to identify these feelings, the more we can determine to let go of our emotional attachment to any situation.

CHAPTER SIX SUMMARY

- It is impossible to live a life without some adversity, obstacles, or pain.

- All people have unconscious "mind chatter." The closer we are to a breakthrough, the louder the "negative mind chatter" becomes. Consider it as a sign that you are getting closer to your objective.

- To get results, we must have in alignment our thoughts, our feelings, and our actions.

- The "void" (also known as the "zone") is the time between the release of an old belief, or way of being, and a rebirth or manifestation of a new belief or way of being.

- Moving beyond our excuses, our fears, and our resistances is the stuff of heroes.

- Be easy with yourself; give yourself a hug. Getting the necessary support is always encouraged.

"Change your thoughts and you change your world."

—Norman Vincent Peale

"We have nothing to fear but fear itself."

—Franklin D. Roosevelt

"To truly forgive is to get to and give up the root of the problem."

—Dr. Steven Barr, acupuncturist

"Never forget that to forgive yourself is to release trapped energy that could be doing good work in the world. Thus, to judge and condemn yourself is a form of selfishness. Self-prosecution is never noble; it does no one a service."

—D. Patrick Miller

Fear of the IRS Audit
By Bob E.

My business was being audited by the IRS. I found it frustrating, exhausting, and time consuming. After a year of this intrusion on my business life, I was guided to write forgiveness affirmations surrounding the obvious upset—the IRS and its auditor assigned to my case—whenever I felt the irritating emotion take over me. I wrote:

I forgive the IRS and Mr. ___ (the auditor's name)

Along with this, I forgave myself, I forgave my business, and I forgave any and all my negative emotions that this situation had brought to the surface within me—the feelings of fear, anxiety, lack, insecurity, and financial concerns. I wrote a few sentences of each, such as:

I forgive myself
I forgive my fear
I forgive my fear and anxiety of money
I forgive my money issues
I forgive my feelings of irritation

Within weeks of my beginning my forgiveness affirmation writings, the auditor was transferred to another case and I received a replacement auditor. This auditor was not only efficient with time, but this auditor found that I was actually owed money by the IRS; I didn't owe the IRS! Now, how good can it get?

Living with an Alcoholic
By Janice

I confided one day to my neighbor Sunnee that I was under enormous stress and strain living with a full-blown alcoholic. My live-in partner's habitual drinking was getting worse by the day. It had gotten to the point that he was drinking a quart of whiskey straight from the bottle every evening when he came home from work. This amount of alcohol, as anyone can imagine, transformed my partner's personality so dramatically that I was looking for a solution to help me move out from under his erratic, controlling, and suppressing behavior. Thoroughly shaken and feeling trapped, I disclosed the deeper complications of my finances, as they were intertwined in a business both my partner and I developed and owned together.

I felt massive fear overcome me each and every day with my partner's out-of-control drinking. My reaction to his irrational behavior seemed to keep me spinning and off balance to the point I could not think rationally or clearly to make any decisions.

So when Sunnee explained to me that I could write forgiveness affirmations and allow the highest and best action to be revealed intuitively to me for my particular situation, I felt I had nothing to lose. I followed through with the suggestions and decided to write the forgiveness affirmations, beginning with my most obvious challenges:

1. my alcoholic partner,
2. my fear,
3. my feelings of no financial support, which would trigger feelings of helplessness.

I feared repercussions from my partner should he discover the papers with my forgiveness writings and that I then would have to deal with more of his irrational rage. Immediately I thought of a solution. Instead of writing forgiveness affirmations on paper, I used a bar of soap as I took my shower each morning and I wrote my affirmations on the shower wall. Each day that I wrote I would visualize all my cares and worries literally being washed down the drain.

In less than three months after I began my forgiveness "soap" writing affirmations, an opportunity to move to another state, to a new home, and start a new life in a new business venture was offered to me with financial start-up money. With greater self-confidence, I left my chaotic lifestyle with no regrets. I later attracted a healthier relationship with a man who was totally supportive in my self-expression. I am forever grateful.

CHAPTER 7

RESPONSES TO COMMONLY ASKED QUESTIONS

How can I forgive someone I absolutely hate?

A person does not have to "like" anyone to begin this forgiveness process. What is necessary, however, is *the willingness to let go.* The person who chooses to write the forgiveness affirmations will automatically benefit by shifting his or her own feelings toward that person. The forgiveness writing process is a proactive step toward releasing our emotional attachment to any person or situation. At the moment a person puts a pen to paper, the facts surrounding the situation will be revealed, and the mind-set of the person writing will improve. The benefits will occur to the writer whether he or she believes in this process or not. This process also works 100 percent better by writing it—not just thinking about it.

It appears to me that if I write forgiveness affirmations, I am focusing on the negative aspects in my life. I believe that "like attracts like" and "whatever you focus upon, you will attract more of it." So how can I do the process that you explain in this book and still feel I'm attracting something positive in my life?

There are two parts to answering this question:

First, a person cannot change what he or she does not acknowledge.

Second, the forgiveness process does not focus on the negative aspect of any situation. It is quite the opposite. It offers a person the ability to determine what is not working in one's own life, letting go of it, and making room for what he or she prefers to experience instead. This *is* the gift a person receives through writing forgiveness affirmations.

If I write on a person who is no longer alive, or on someone I have no way of contacting, will this process work for me?

Yes. The forgiveness process will always benefit the person who is choosing to perform this forgiveness technique.

Is this book based on any particular religion?

No. This process does not follow any particular belief or faith. Forgiveness is free to all who wish to experience its benefits.

Can you explain what you mean by saying forgiveness is a "Universal Truth"?

Through research and discovery, you will find forgiveness teachings revealed in the Christian Bible, New Age materials, the Koran, Sikhism, Jainism, Judaism, Taoism, Confucianism, the Twelve-Step anonymous programs, and in the works of numerous authors, poets, and columnists, to name just a few.

This forgiveness writing technique is so simple, it sounds too good to be true, so how can it be effective?

Writing forgiveness affirmations sounds very simple, and the writing method requires very little effort. Yet people who have not made an effort to even try this process are unable to experience the profound effect it can have on their lives. This process is customized when each individual physically performs the writing method to achieve the most effective results. In other words, the process appears simple, yet it remains profoundly effective.

What is the best time to write forgiveness affirmations?

The optimal time for anyone to write is a time when he or she will not be disturbed by interruptions such as the telephone, television, radio, or daily distractions. Many people find they love to write in the quiet of the morning or in the evening, right before bedtime. Each person needs to find his or her own quiet space, and time, that works best for that person.

How many times would you suggest a person write forgiveness affirmations on a particular person, or situation, to get results?

People need to write as many times as it takes for them to attain a sense of peace. Only they will know that answer, simply by the way they feel. Some people feel immediate changes from writing only one or two forgiveness affirmations. For others, it may take several pages of written affirmations over a long time.

How does one know when he or she has written enough forgiveness affirmations?

These three aspects of writing forgiveness will become apparent.

1. Previously unknown facts surrounding the circumstance will be revealed.

2. The actions necessary will become known to you.

3. The circumstances for the person writing forgiveness affirmations will improve.

Will I experience any physical symptoms because of writing?

Possibly. You may experience some physical discomfort such as writer's cramp in your hand, backaches, headaches, nervous tension, muscle tension, bodily aches, increased elimination, or other physical discomforts. These symptoms can be signs of suppressed feelings trying to come to the surface. If the symptoms persist, either you can continue to write despite them, or momentarily discontinue writing until the symptoms subside. Then resume writing as you feel the need.

Will "thinking" these forgiveness affirmations work just as well as writing them?

Yes and no. Through the years, people who have written down their affirmations have greatly accelerated their forgiveness process. If for whatever reason they were unable to do the writing, they believed that "thinking" their forgiveness was better than to do nothing at all.

Does it matter if I write my forgiveness affirmations with either a pencil or pen?

It does not appear to matter which handwriting medium one chooses to use. Children have used chalk and crayons on sidewalks. A person wrote affirmations using a stick in the sand on a beach. People have written on napkins with a pen in restaurants. One woman wrote while showering, using a bar of soap on her shower wall to write out her affirmations. In all these cases the forgiveness affirmation process was successful. Use any writing tool that's comfortable for you. You can write anywhere, at any time.

Does writing forgiveness affirmations on a computer or a typewriter work as well as handwriting?

A typewriter or a computer does not appear to give the best results. Our emotions tend to be reflected in our handwriting. The typewriter and computer are unable to transfer emotions in the same way. Certain parts of the brain are stimulated and trigger random thoughts when we write by hand. This is necessary to the forgiveness process. When you use a typewriter or computer you are not creating the same brain response. Science has proven a person will use a different part of his or her brain when typing than when writing by hand. To receive the maximum benefit, I highly recommend that you handwrite your affirmations with whatever handwriting tool you are most comfortable using.

What do you recommend I do with my written affirmation papers after I've completed them?

Most of us will consider our written affirmations as confidential and private. You have several choices of what to do with the papers.

For some the physical act of tearing up the papers gives them a sense of tearing up their problem and releasing it by throwing the pieces away. Others create a ritual by burning the papers and visualizing their problem going up in smoke. Still others will use a forgiveness journal and save the writings to review later, so they can monitor their results.

What is imperative is that we release our attachment to that which was written. Do whatever feels best for you and allows you to feel you have completely "let go."

Can I do this writing process once and be done with it for life?

Yes. However, it will depend on how you feel about your situation. If a life-challenging issue persists, or recurs, it is highly recommended that you continue to write. I think of the forgiving process as being like a stack of plates in a cafeteria; when you remove the top plate another plate appears. Or think of it as being like an onion. You remove the outer layers; there is another layer then to be removed. So to answer your question, it is a process. It is ongoing as long as we have a body. I will practice forgiving in any area (with any person, place, thing, or situation/circumstance) that upsets my peace of mind and my ability to be genuine. It gives you the power to change, including ending your relationship with the person you forgive.

While writing forgiveness affirmations on one particular issue, all of a sudden, from out of nowhere, another issue surfaced in my mind. This new issue appears to be unrelated to what I was originally writing about. What does this mean?

This is a common occurrence. Our minds are designed to think in this way. When we clear one thought, another thought wants to come into our awareness to fill the void. This is why it is suggested that you write in a quiet space. The silence allows our minds to begin recalling past experiences. This phenomenon is a natural gift that will ultimately help in the forgiveness process. These new thoughts can allow us to release the memories that have kept us trapped in repetitive patterns that no longer serve us.

Can you use this writing method to control or manipulate the results?

People who think that they can control or manipulate their situation with this writing process would most likely not bring about a positive change in their circumstances. That isn't what forgiveness is about. The process of forgiveness focuses on releasing and letting go. A need to control is not releasing and letting go. One of the major aspects of forgiveness is having no attachment to the outcome. It takes courage to write forgiveness and to allow the truth to surface. Be prepared to accept whatever happens as being in the highest and best good for all concerned.

Additional Comments about the Writing Process

Affirmation writing is not about neatness, spelling, grammar, or length. Any style of writing will get results. Relax—no forgiveness police will spell check or grammatically correct your writing.

Find the writing style that works best for you. The following example illustrates this point.

A married couple began writing using the simple one-line format:

"I forgive_____"

The husband continued to find that writing the one-line format worked for him. On the other hand, his wife became highly expressive and now writes entire paragraphs. However, in either case, they always begin with the words "I forgive."

Whatever style works for you is correct. It is recommended that you begin each of your writing affirmations with the words "I forgive."

"When you are inspired by some great purpose, some extraordinary project, all your thoughts break their bonds; your mind transcends limitations, your consciousness expands in every direction, and you

find yourself in a new, great and wonderful world. Dormant forces, faculties and talents become alive, and you discover yourself to be a greater person by far than you ever dreamed yourself to be."

—Patanjali (c. 1st to 3rd century BC)

CHAPTER 8

INTRODUCTION TO
WRITING PREFORGIVENESS

Preforgiveness is choosing to be proactive instead of reactive. Writing preforgiveness sets the stage for diffusing stresses, fears, and/or anxieties associated with any anticipated problem(s), both known and unknown, associated with a future event connected to any person, any place, or any situation. The intent is to neutralize the stress before you encounter the actual emotion-triggering person, place, or situation that may occur in future time. By writing preforgiveness affirmations, you will discover and experience how doing so supports your living in the present moment. Living in the "now" allows you to be guided by your intuitive self, which will guide you to the highest and right actions.

The following is a list of possible circumstances that you may consider writing preforgiveness affirmations on:

Before you date
Before you marry

Before family reunions

Before births/weddings/funerals

Before holiday gatherings/celebrations

Before adoption situations

Before meeting with a separated partner

Before meeting with divorced partners

Before gatherings with stepfamilies

Before job interviews, before hiring

Before work performance reviews

Before tests

Before school reunions

Before making important investments

Before meeting with clients

Before buying or selling anything

Before requesting a loan

Before giving speeches or presentations

Before meetings with legal council

Before court trials and/or a sentencing

Before signing legal papers

Before vacations

Before traveling

Before arriving at the airport

Before operations/surgeries

Before appointments

This list names only a few possible situations for which a person may consider writing preforgiveness affirmations.

The procedure for writing preforgiveness is the same as for writing forgiveness affirmations that you found in Chapter 3. The only difference is that the writing is on a potential future situation that is creating an upset in one's mind. The following is an example of writing a preforgiveness affirmation:

Let us use the situation of attending a future event, a planned family reunion. Apply the power of a written affirmation using the words "family reunion" since the very thought of this occasion is causing your stress.

Taking pen and paper in hand, write your first preforgiveness affirmation as follows. Write the words "I forgive" followed by the words "family reunion." You are choosing to defuse what could be a potential future stressful situation. For example, write:

"I forgive the <u>family reunion</u>"

You do not have to write the words "I preforgive" as a beginning phrase. You have only to use the words "I forgive." Again, writing these two words begins the process of erasing our stress when we feel it starts to overwhelm us.

You will make the decision of whether to visit this future planned family reunion or not by reconnecting to your intuitive, authentic self after writing. You will know what is in your highest and best interest by the intuitive feelings you get. Following your "intuitive prompts," those "gut feelings" otherwise known as your "first impressions," is a sign that you are in the flow of life.

Additional Examples of Preforgiveness Affirmations Writings on People, Places, Things, or Situations

Person: Writing preforgiveness before meeting with a certain person.

"I forgive <u>having to meet Uncle Joe</u>"

Place: Writing preforgiveness before an operation in the hospital.

"I forgive <u>my hospital and staff</u>"

Thing: Writing preforgiveness before taking a test.

"I forgive <u>my entrance exam to college</u>"

Situation: Writing preforgiveness on a personal and emotionally triggered situation.

"I forgive <u>my divorce settlement</u>"

Master the possibilities of setting yourself up for success by practicing preforgiveness. I liken preforgiveness to buying an extra insurance policy when I need it most.

You are guaranteeing the facts of a situation to be honest and truthful. If there is a potential problem, those facts will often be revealed to you and the actions to take will also be made known. Take notice of what you are attracting into your life. Become more aware of answers being supplied to you, possibly through a book you are reading, or through talking with a stranger, or through a radio program you are listening to. You are creating and improving your life circumstances simply by stating and focusing on what you prefer instead (review Chapter 5, "What Do You Prefer Instead?"). You will experience a bonus in just experiencing less of an emotional impact. Quite often, and more times than not, the circumstances will shift to be in your best interest if you continue writing on your situation.

"In everyone's life, at some time, our inner fire goes out. It is then burst into flame by an encounter with another human being. We should all be thankful for those people who rekindle the inner spirit."

—Albert Schweitzer

Preforgiveness, Custody, and Child Support
By J. D.

I was separated from my wife and two children. My soon-to-be-ex-wife wanted more child support, more than was agreed upon by the two of us, even when we used a court-assigned marriage mediator. I literally did not have an extra dime to my name and was parenting my children a few days of the week as the soon-to-be-ex-wife allowed.

I wrote forgiveness affirmations on her and I wrote forgiveness affirmations on myself the night before the courtroom date that would decide my fate regarding custody of my two boys and the child-support amounts.

In the courtroom the next day, the soon-to-be-ex-wife's lawyer told the judge why I should pay more in child support and asked for full custody to go to the children's mother only.

When it came time to present my case, I stood up nervously as I was representing myself. It was if something other than me began to speak through me. I asked the judge point-blank, I asked the court why, when I was not a deadbeat dad, would the courts take the privilege of their father's love and guidance away from his children? I also brought paperwork as proof that I could not pay more, plain and simple. The paper proved I not withholding money to spite my soon-to-be-ex-wife.

The judge heard my heartfelt plea for shared custody. The judge heard the truth and saw the facts. The judge saw through the lawyer's reasoning and accusations of my being an irresponsible father. The judge gave me shared half time and ended up decreasing the child-support payments. The judge stated and it was recorded that the soon-to-be-ex-wife was using her own children to obtain money she did not deserve. I could hardly believe what I was hearing.

I understand that no one wins in a divorce, especially our children. Yet I witnessed justice rule and now I can get back to the job of being a dad.

CHAPTER 9

FORGIVENESS SUCCESS STORIES

In the stories that follow and in those that appeared earlier in these pages, a few names have been changed to protect the privacy of the people giving their true accounts. These represent just a tiny sample of the stories that have been relayed to me during the last twenty-plus years to demonstrate the power of forgiveness in action. Enjoy.

A New Lease on Family Life
By Victoria Pratt

I found the forgiveness exercises changed my life within a few days of writing forgiveness. About a year and a half ago, I had been expecting my sister Cindy to come visit me from the East Coast, and I had told her when I would have some time off to spend with her, and she told me when she was planning to arrive in town. After that, I made plans around her schedule to go visit our other sister at a different time. Cindy is not always easy to get along with and has alienated everyone else in the family with her accusations of their not doing enough for her and blame for being cold toward her. Well, either accidentally or not, she booked tickets to come during the week I wasn't going to be home! When I told her that I'd be gone that week, she flew into a rage, which is something that she can do without too much provocation, and said I had deliberately done this, deliberately dropped my plans to be with her, which was far from the truth. I usually put out a lot of effort to make her feel loved and welcomed, and I have defended her to the others in the family for years, saying she's just insecure, dealing with a lot, and so on. She literally screamed at me into the phone for about ten minutes and ended up saying that she would not visit me and could not tolerate such behavior. Then she hung up on me.

Cindy came out West and visited other people but never called me, not for more than a year. She had not been on speaking terms with others in the family, but she had always been OK with me until this incident. I was hurt that she had assumed I would callously ignore our plans to get together, and I was bewildered that she went immediately into a rage instead of trying to figure out some solution.

A year or so later, Cindy called my daughter when I happened to be with her. The phone was handed to me, and we unexpectedly had to talk to each other. Again, the anger and accusations came out, with tears and yelling. I couldn't even make her hear that I had arranged my schedule *around* hers, and that I would not drop my plans to be with her, that I wouldn't do that to anyone. (*Least* of all her!) I was angry that she thought I could be so uncaring. She was taking out anger about other things on me, and I had done nothing to deserve it. I figured I was better off not hearing from her.

She didn't call me back, but a few months later, my dad called to tell me that Cindy was coming out to visit within the month, and he told me the dates. I didn't want another scene, and I didn't know how to get through the anger and frustration I was feeling. I didn't want another screaming fight.

I remembered my friend Sunnee's talking about forgiveness and decided to call her to find out more about it, since I was not succeeding on my own. She told me to just start writing forgiveness—even if you don't totally feel it, start writing, "I forgive you for screaming. I forgive you for being afraid. I forgive you for not trusting." I didn't think there were so many things to write about, but soon I was filling pages every day. And of course, I also had to forgive myself for getting myself into difficult situations and quite a few other things.

Within a couple of days, I felt a huge weight lift. I didn't feel as if I had to "fix" anybody any

more. I didn't have to work it out with anyone;
I just forgave. And forgave. I found I was able to
let go of the anger. I realized that the screaming
and the lack of trust came out of fear, fear of loss.
I understand that one. I didn't need to be angry
at her, or anyone. I needed only to take care of
myself. It was a huge relief.

When my sister finally called me again, which was
a few weeks later, to my amazement she apologized,
saying she had been really upset about other things
and had jumped to the wrong conclusion. She said
she loved me and was looking forward to seeing
me. I couldn't believe it, because other family rifts
had been going on for years with other family
members and were still unresolved.

Cindy came and she and her kids spent time
with me and we actually had a sweet visit. She didn't
get into all the "negative family stuff" that she had
usually complained about—another amazement.
I know that I can let go of the anger I had and
accept the relationship the way it is. I know that I
am not without faults, and I can forgive myself, as
I am also still learning.

I guess the bottom line is that we are all
unfinished products, still learning, and all of us
can be forgiven for the fear, the anger, the mistrust,
the unkind words, or whatever we do to express

our deepest feelings. I have written forgiveness toward my parents, all my siblings, my friends, my ex-husband, and all the people who are important to me for all the things I felt were not right. I guess I let go of blaming them and feeling wronged or victimized by their actions. And of course, I had to forgive myself for being angry, for misunderstanding, for not taking care of myself, for being selfish, and so on. There are so many ways that we are not perfect. And maybe that actually is perfection, the process, the growth, the willingness to learn. And the willingness to forgive. It certainly freed my mind from the tangles of anger and bitterness. I'm still "writing forgiveness." It is an ongoing process, one that gives me real peace of mind. Thank you, Sunnee, for this gift.

Forgiveness Is Blessedness
By Michael Anthony

When I started writing forgiveness, I was told two things: Whatever you write about will reveal its truth, and it will get better or the problem will go away. Well, amen. With time I knew truths that scared me. And, yes, it got better and the problem shifted to the point that it went away.

Forgiveness opened the path to my own heart, to who I really am. Through the truth of my own self, I was able to work forgiveness with myself. This was most important for me because self-forgiveness opened the door for me to open forgiveness with the rest of my life.

I wrote forgiveness affirmations on friends, family, my business, myself, health, and many other things. I was not saying all these things were wrong; it is just a way for me to clear the path for these things to manifest in my life the way I wanted them to.

Forgiveness has led me to a path of gratitude. My life is so blessed that I am in disbelief much of the time. I sometimes wonder if God ever thinks about anyone else! It is through forgiveness that I am able to stay in constant breath with the God I love.

I find myself after two years of writing that I write only as I need it. It is not as constant as when I started but I will use it as a lifetime tool.

Legal Challenge
By Michael Stevens

When my business partner and I were being wrongfully sued for embezzlement, writing forgiveness remarkably changed our situation.

After working two years for a company as bookkeepers, my partner and I found out that the person we were working for was not the owner of the company. The real owner showed up on the scene and accused everyone who was working there of embezzling money. My partner and I were innocent but we were being sued by the owner even though we were just independent contractors. We were being sued for $250,000 and didn't know what to do. My partner and I both began writing forgiveness on our situation. Within days of writing forgiveness we were led to the perfect attorney for our situation. Up to that point we felt helpless and fearful but the action of getting just the right attorney to do the job was nothing short of a miracle, since we had only a matter of days to acquire one.

After three months of deliberation passed, the owner who was suing us dropped the case for no apparent reason and we were exonerated of the crime. We, as partners, said that the only thing that got us through the ordeal was that every time we felt stressed or anxious about any aspect of this situation, the forgiveness writing got us through it. We still thank Sunnee to this day for showing us this simple forgiveness writing process.

Career Changes and Forgiveness
By M. Kane

I was becoming increasingly dissatisfied with my position at work. Instead of quitting my job, as I was considering doing, I chose instead to write forgiveness affirmations on my career as Sunnee suggested. I wrote the words, "*I forgive my career*" several times on a piece of paper for several days in a row. Within weeks, I was promoted to manager of a newly created department designed just for me. Obviously my circumstances improved. I am totally in love with what I am doing and I feel successful!

Single Mother, Flat Tire, and Stressed
by the Extra Expense
By Kathleen Jensen

My boys and I drove up to my sister's house in Nevada City for the New Year's weekend. The next day I realized that my back tire was completely flat. I was very stressed because I did not know how that with this flat tire I was going to get my car in to the shop to have the tire repaired or to buy a new tire. I was also very concerned about the money that could be involved with buying a new tire.

My sister Lori told me about her friend Sunnee and the technique of writing forgiveness. That night I wrote forgiveness on the flat tire that caused me to be so upset. The next day my brother-in-law Ken came home and was able to put enough air into my tire that I could drive it into town to a tire shop, which could evaluate if I needed to replace the tire or repair it if possible.

As it turned out I did not have to buy a new tire; the repair shop was able to fix my tire and *it did this free of charge*. This was a special gift to me as money was very tight.

Improved Family Relationships
By Cathy O'Connor

For the last two years I have practiced "forgiveness writing" as suggested by Sunnee. To my amazement I am able to have new relationships with family and friends that were blocked by unresolved issues, either on my part or from the other person. I come from a traditional Irish/Italian Catholic family that is riddled with addiction issues and so on.

One of my greatest blocks was with one of my brothers and his wife. My brother sexually molested me when I was very young (he is eight years my senior; I was about five years old). Although I never confronted my brother face to face, I did do a lot of spiritual work as well as traditional counseling, hypnotherapy, and so on. The unresolved issue with my brother affected all my relationships, romantic and basic friendships, because of my inability to trust. He married when I was sixteen. His wife and I had a good relationship, or so I thought, until the last ten years. She outwardly degrades me and so on, for what reason I do not know.

I started to write forgiveness affirmations on both of them (as well as on any and all situations that caused me any signs of stress). Now I feel at peace. My brother now will try to contact me; before this we would avoid each other. He is open, and I think he wants to know what is different about me. His wife still keeps her distance.

I am able to be in a room with my family and feel at peace in the core of my being. In moments I may have trepidation; however, when I write forgiveness and release it to the universe, my energy and my intention change. This also creates space for new kinds of people to be in my life.

This experience is invaluable to me because it is a tool that creates energy change, an intention shift, a cellular vibrational change that ultimately brings me back to my Source. The unlimited experience of spirit and higher purpose is true freedom!

Thank you, Sunnee, for inspiring me to be all that I desire. Without forgiveness, I would continue to drink the poison of anger and resentment hoping the other person would die. Blessings to you.

Facing Court for Revoked Driver's License, City Parking Tickets
By Christopher V. B.

As a young man in my late twenties, living in a metropolitan area, I had accumulated numerous unpaid city parking tickets. The worst of my predicament was that my driver's license had also been revoked because of several speeding tickets. I took my chances and continued to drive, knowing it was illegal to drive without a license.

I learned the process of how to write forgiveness affirmations when Sunnee presented her material at my church.

With all the courage I could muster, I decided to face the consequences of my actions (or lack of) in court regarding my driver's license and parking tickets. I asked Sunnee if she would write the forgiveness affirmations during my time in the courtroom. My mind was racing with thoughts of pending doom for my negligent behavior and thinking that the worst would happen when I did go to court—possible jail time?

I did my best not to appear nervous in the court, waiting to hear my name to be called before the judge. All the while Sunnee focused on writing forgiveness affirmations on the presiding judge, the court reporter, the town, the parking and speeding tickets, my revoked driver's license, and myself of course.

In short, the final outcome was that I had to pay a total of $110. All my city parking tickets were erased by the judge and my driver's license was restored that day. I felt a huge weight lift from my shoulders. I learned the power of forgiveness and to accept responsibility for my behavior by not allowing any of this to happen again.

Money Lost by the Delivery Service
By Wendy Scott

I found out how well writing forgiveness works when my check for $2,000 that I sent to my sister Berna to help her buy a car was lost through the FedEx delivery service. I immediately stopped payment on the check. The bank held the check for the next ninety days before I was credited the full $2,000 amount.

Meanwhile, I learned a big lesson about myself as I went through all the extra time and money in trying to retrieve it. I wrote forgiveness affirmations on my sister. I realized after writing that I felt I *had an obligation* to take care of my older sister and I resented it. My sister got along fine without my financial help.

Later that week, I was in a casino and I hit the royal flush and won $1,600. When I talked to Berna, she said that she had been praying that whole time to bless me for doing such a kind deed even though the money never arrived for her. I felt that my writing forgiveness and my sister's prayer were both answered.

Moving the Energy, Feeling Good
By Janet Scott

I am on my third day of writing forgiveness affirmations and I have had some wonderful revelations and wanted to share them with you. First of all, after doing the forgiveness writing, I arrived home and my partner was more affectionate toward me. Yesterday, while I was doing the writing, a flash of Jesus's words about forgiving seventy times seven came to me. I decided to write my forgiveness words seventy times a day for seven days.

Then I began to sing the affirmations as I wrote them each time. Wow, I feel that as I write, and more thoughts come up, it is as if I am releasing hooks in myself. The energy around me is freeing up immensely. The universe is increasing my supply already. The bits of energy I have been holding to, this stuck garbage, is moving! Yesterday, I had three-and-a-half-hour clients and earned great money. I can see how the "stuckness" has been holding me back. Thank you, thank you, thank you for sharing this gift with me. I appreciate it immensely.

Out of Work and the Rent Is Due
By Morgan le Faye

Because of an injury at work, I found myself not able to work and create an income, and I was unable to sustain workers' compensation for more than a year. Still injured, with minimal income, I found myself going into debt fast.

My situation paralyzed me in fear. I had no family to which I could turn, no place to go. At times the fear was so great, I didn't have the strength to fight my way out of a paper bag. I would freeze every time I looked at the bills stacking up. It was as if I were wrapped in a ball of yarn. I felt cornered and I was scared.

Without my health, I felt I had nothing. I was up against the wall. Whenever my fear surfaced and it roared its ugly head, I would write in my forgiveness journal as Sunnee had suggested.

"I forgive my fear"
"I forgive my lack of money"
"I forgive not having an income"
"I forgive my fear of being homeless"
"I forgive my fear of being abandoned"
"I would forgive 'I was at the very end and at the very bottom'"

I wrote on anything that made me feel uncomfortable.

I also wrote forgiveness on my landlord off and on for more than a year. I so feared that I would be evicted from my apartment because of the rent's being late or not being paid.

I learned by forgiving that life will show you the gift in whatever you are experiencing. In my case, I was learning to trust; forgiving made me reach out to people and *ask* for help.

That life lesson was at my door when the landlord came to collect rent one day during the Christmas holidays. This was the first time I did not have rent money. I told him the truth. I had been injured at work. A lawsuit was pending, but I could not pay and I apologized for not being able to. The landlord told me not to worry because he had been up against this himself several years ago; he said he understood! I cried and cried from relief.

Miracles kept happening for me as I continued to write forgiveness affirmations. I was explaining my problem to my hairdresser (we had a barter agreement that Christmas; I made her custom jewelry to sell in her shop or give away in exchange for my haircuts). Again I did not have the month's rent money. My hairdresser asked me how much my rent was, to which I replied, $1,000. My hairdresser wrote the check in my landlord's name and paid my rent. No words can describe how appreciative I was to receive the emotional and financial support.

Months and months later, my landlord called and said, "I will have to evict you." I immediately wrote forgiveness affirmations on my fear of eviction. With a clearer mind, I got the idea to open my apartment and sell my handmade jewelry and my treasured rock collection. People not only came to buy these items from me; they even brought food to feed me. Many brought me department-store gift cards so I could buy items I might need. Neighbors brought $100 cash envelopes and left them for me. Again and again, I heard how *I had inspired them* by what I was going through!

I also received a much-desired jewelry class paid for in full by workers' compensation so that I could increase my skills in creating specialized, one-of-a-kind jewelry. One of the instructors in this school seemed to give me a hard time in the classroom. Again, Sunnee suggested that I write preforgiveness affirmations on the instructor before returning to class. The next day, the teacher treated me like the "gem" of the class, as if I were the only one in the classroom.

When it came time to attend my workers' compensation claim settlement hearing, I wrote ten to fifteen minutes of forgiveness affirmations in the courtroom on my lawyer, the court clerks, the judge, and the lawyer for the workers' compensation insurance company. The final outcome shifted in my favor. The insurance lawyers actually offered and reduced a couple of thousand of dollars in liens. Within thirty minutes I was awarded thousands of dollars when I had expected nothing financially.

I found that forgiveness breaks through the fear; it sets you free. When I write forgiveness, it clears my mind of mental blocks and frees the space for energy to flow.

In summary, "When we allow people or situations to upset us, we are allowing them to live rent free in our heads."

Weight Issues and Menopause
By Beth Lynne

I found myself overweight by more than twenty-five pounds. Never having had a weight issue before this, I was in a quandary as to what I needed to do. Everything I had done when I was younger appeared to not have been working for me for the last five years.

I wrote forgiveness affirmations such as:

"I forgive my weight"
"I forgive my weight"

It was as if a dam broke, and from that moment I became like a magnet for solutions that were right, correct, and suitable for my life.

First, I attracted into my awareness a natural solution for my menopausal symptoms and within months I was feeling better. I also followed through with a hunch that my thyroid was low, and after being tested, I also acquired a perfect solution for that. Now, feeling motivated, I am back exercising.

As I continued to write forgiveness on whatever was obviously an obstacle, I allowed it to lead me where I needed to go. In less than a year, I have an internal motivator for all the right actions to basically revamp myself with new clothes, new haircut, and new style that I could easily afford. Needless to say, I feel confident and beautiful at this stage of my life.

Cleaning My Closet
By Sandía Borden

Sunnee Roman's forgiveness program amazes me. Not entirely sure how open I was to this concept, I followed her directions. I thought I had only four or five people to forgive but my list ended up with at least forty people from the beginning of my time. After writing, "I forgive you, _____ _____," as Sunnee suggested, I found I had to add a little more for some people. "I forgive you, _____, for not loving me" was the general addition. I discovered a trend and from that point on understood what bothered me consciously and unconsciously, which gave me a tool to help work these things through.

Having "cleaned my closet," as Sunnee would say, by finishing my forgiveness list, I sat and attempted to fill it with good things before the bad things could collect again.

I needed a car desperately. I made a list: This car must be safe, reliable, and affordable. Within a week someone offered me a car—safe, reliable, affordable, and I could make payments.

I needed a new job. I wanted a job in which I could use and exercise my brain, with some research involved, detail oriented, and people I would love working with. Within a few weeks I got that job and I look forward to going to work every day.

I lost my sweet Queensland heeler, my "little sister" as I called her. When I was ready to look for a new puppy, I made my list again—brains, energy, loyalty, beauty, and love. Within a week a litter of border collie puppies was advertised in our local newspaper. I went to just look and immediately fell in love with one beautiful puppy and took her home. It was love at first sight. She has all the attributes I asked for and more.

So many very positive things have happened for me since I attended Sunnee's forgiveness workshop; these are only a few that meant a lot to me and really affected my quality of life.

A Client's Custom Home and the Architectural Board, Story Number One
By Sunnee K. Roman

A client and her architect went before the architectural board for her first review of the plans for her custom $1 million home that was to be built in a very chic neighborhood. This client had heard many horror stories from the neighbors who had already built custom homes in the area. Many told this client how they had to get lawyers to fight for months before they could get their homes passed by the board.

That very evening, while waiting for the client's name to be called before the board for review of her home plans, we observed the architectural board discussing for half an hour whether to pass a sign designed for a local business. This request for a business sign was not only turned down the month before, it was turned down again that evening, and the business owner would have to return for a third time the following month.

Starting to get nervous as I thought about the architectural board's turning down approval on a little sign for the town, I heard little voices in my head wondering how would they treat us for an entire house!

I focused on writing forgiveness affirmations on the obvious people involved, which naturally would be the client, the architect, the town, the architectural board members, and myself, along with any other thoughts that may have surfaced while writing. I set the intention for this meeting to go as smoothly as possible for the client and the architectural board.

In less than fifteen minutes, the architectural board gave its approval with a few suggestions and passed this client's home plans. The architectural board even complimented her on a wonderful design and joyfully bantered among themselves. Needless to say, we were all thrilled by the outcome.

Home Contractor/Builder and the Architectural Board, Story Number Two
By Sunnee K. Roman

An architect designed a custom, $2 million spec home as requested by a licensed builder/contractor. The contractor owned the property, which was in a very posh, exclusive neighborhood with few opportunities left to build.

After six months of reviewing the contractor's plans, the small town's architectural board would not approve of and/or pass the contractor's plans for what seemed small and petty reasons (such as not showing a shower door or a shower rod on the custom home plan).

Losing money, even though all legal building codes and requests were upheld, the builder/ contractor now felt his hands were tied; he didn't know what to do, and it was costing him a lot of money every time the project was delayed.

It is now the seventh month, the seventh meeting before the town's architectural board. The contractor and the architect were available for the meeting.

I began writing forgiveness affirmations on the obvious, which were all those involved, including the contractor/builder, the architect, the names that were displayed on the nameplates in front of each architectural board member. I included the name of the town and anything that may have popped into my mind during my writing. I continued to write on each person throughout the evening as we waited our turn to be called before the board. I held the intention of moving beyond the invisible block that was keeping this committee from giving the contractor/builder approval of his home plans.

Within minutes after we were called before the board to review the home plans, the person in charge of the building committee said, "To tell you the truth, if it was up to me I would never pass these plans. Yet these plans meet all legal requirements and so I must pass them."

That evening the facts surfaced about what was blocking the committee's approval; it showed up as one board member's personal reasons. Writing forgiveness affirmations on this situation bypassed the block. The builder/contractor's home plans were approved that evening.

A Priest's Confession
By Sunnee K. Roman

A priest was visiting one of the guests at the retirement center where I worked. One day, the priest stopped me in the hallway and we had a very nice chat. As I was not raised Catholic, I asked the priest what the Catholic church taught regarding the subject of forgiveness. He did not answer me; instead he asked me for my phone number and address and made an appointment to speak with me the following week.

This priest drove more than two hours from where he lived to my home. We talked about the forgiveness process that I was doing, how it had been working for me, and about others who had practiced this method of writing and their miracles. He agreed after a few hours to try writing forgiveness affirmations too.

On his second visit to my home, the priest began to tell me about his past, about losing his parents through a tragic car accident when he was very young, and about how those who became his caretakers had molested him. You could see the anguish in his face, as if the pain had never healed.

On the third visit, the priest told me he was leaving the priesthood and moving onward in his life. I was shocked at such a quick decision. He also confessed that in the Catholic order he was leaving, child molesting was taking place with some of the altar boys.

That was the last I saw of the priest. I read in the local paper shortly afterward that there was an investigation and legal actions were taken. This was the time of my own heightened awareness of how powerful the forgiveness affirmations can be and how you can believe "The Three" will occur:

1. The facts are revealed.

2. The actions necessary will be made known.

3. The circumstances will improve.

A Fed-Up-with-Life Story
By Ria Bacigalupa

I was introduced to Sunnee Roman and her message of forgiveness during a point in my life when I really needed it, although I didn't think so at the time. I had just quit my long-held job because of a stinging betrayal by both a coworker and my boss and I was devastated and lost. Forgiving them was the last thing that I wanted to do but the friend who invited me to my first forgiveness workshop knew better.

At that point in my life, the job catastrophe was just another bad experience in a long string of bad experiences and I was fed up with my life, myself, and the entire universe. I literally hated pretty much everyone and everything. Thanks to my friend who had invited me to the workshop, I was starting to awaken again after a long period of spiritual inactivity. Although I was reluctant to accept the invitation, I figured I had nothing to lose and I was willing to at least go and check it out.

So I showed up and took a seat after experiencing a few synchronicities about the topic of forgiveness. I was reading a lot of spiritual books and it seemed as if everything I picked up talked about the need to forgive. I was very impressed with Sunnee herself. She is so upbeat and incredibly passionate and overall just a beautiful person, obviously loving life. I wanted to love my life too so I paid attention even though I was still hesitant about the whole topic.

I gave it a try. At first, I just did a sentence here and a sentence there, remembering what she said about not having to like the person, just having to forgive them. I liked that part a lot. I didn't have to like people who had wronged me but I could still forgive them! That made it easier. One night I decided that I needed to forgive everyone and everything if I were ever to move on and be happy with myself. I needed to let go of a lot of stuff that was dragging me down. So I started writing. It turned into a sort of word association. Each topic/word I thought of and forgave in writing led to the next one. It was like an avalanche. I wrote for hours and forgave every little thing and person I could possibly think of until I couldn't think of anything else and the associations stopped.

When I woke up the next morning it was as if a dam had broken. All that writing had created a huge energetic shift in me that I could really feel. I started writing in my journal about this feeling. At some point, the writing changed and turned into an automatic-writing experience. I was receiving guidance through the words on the page and they were not coming from me! I had never experienced anything like this before. The language changed, the tone changed, and I started writing directive sentences telling me how I could view the situation about quitting my job and my life in general. It was very pertinent, very loving, individual guidance and it helped me immensely. This divine energy communicating through my hand told me to listen only to myself and to my heart, not to anyone else. Other people may have good intentions but their egos usually get in the way. It was a true revelation! I looked back on my life at all the people whom I had looked to for guidance instead of deciding for myself what was right—my ex-boss being one of the biggest ones. It dawned on me how other people's advice had usually sent me down the wrong path. It was based on what they wanted, not necessarily what was truly good for me, and I had blindly followed it many times. The times that I had listened only to myself, things usually turned out well.

From that day on, I stopped looking outside myself for answers and my life has gotten exponentially better. I trust myself and for the first time in my life I truly love myself. From everything I have studied, I have finally learned to let go and trust the universe even when things are hard. It has made all the difference in the world. I try to remember to do forgiveness work whenever something is bothering me and I feel stuck. For me, it has been invaluable. It works because it allows you to let go of sticky issues that always lurk under the surface. It allows stagnant, negative energy to start moving again and that is the key. From there anything and everything is possible!

Sometimes, I do still find it hard to forgive. I think everyone does. What I try to remember is that harboring unforgiveness is hurting *me* the most. I am the one who carries around the constant resentment and that built-up resentment will only hurt me in the long run, in any number of ways. I am no longer interested in hurting myself. I did that for too many years. I am finally happy with myself and believe I deserve only the best in life and that is truly extraordinary! Thank you, Sunnee!

"Forgiveness work has had a profound effect on me. I am continuously discovering how it is showing up in my life. It is the easiest and most satisfying way to move from feeling like a victim to feeling empowered."

—Lori Burkart Frank, CPCC (Certified Professional Coactive Coach)

NOTES

Chapter 3

1. Richards, Deb. (2005, November 10). The pen is mightier. *Sydney (Australia) Morning Herald,* p. 6.

2. Lemus, Frankie D., MA. (2006, Winter.) Change is good. *Paradigm,* 8–10.

3. Pennebaker, James W., and Beall, Sandra Klihr. (1986). Confronting a traumatic event: Toward an understanding of inhibition and disease. *Journal of Abnormal Psychology, 95,* 274–281.

4. Wellner, Alison Stein. (2003, March 1). *American demographics: The new science of focus groups.* Retrieved August 27, 2007, from http://www.acxiom.com/default.aspx?ID=2123&DisplayID=119

Chapter 6

5. McGraw, Phil, Dr. *Marriage and divorce: The statistics.* Retrieved August 27, 2007, from http://www.drphil.com/articles/article/351

6. Hendrix, Harville, PhD. (1988). *Getting the love you want: A guide for couples.* New York: Henry Holt.

ACKNOWLEDGMENTS

I acknowledge and thank the people too numerous to mention in this book who crossed my path, trusting in and practicing this writing process. I so appreciate hearing your personal "aha!" moments, the successful life shifts you created for yourselves regardless of circumstances. Your stories and questions provided the fuel for putting this knowledge into book form.

I wish to acknowledge my two children, Justin and Jacinda. At the ages of twelve and nine, they were the first children to use this forgiveness process. They did so, even during what seemed to be insurmountable family challenges at the time. No words can express how grateful I am for their incredible faith, courage, and belief in me and in this forgiveness process.

I offer special thanks to my partner and friend, Tom, for his great patience and the numerous levels of support during the years of research for this book. Without your backing, I would not have had the freedom necessary to bring this book to fruition.

Loving gratitude toward my parents for giving me the gift of life. An extra portion of appreciation toward my mother, who contributed courage, fortitude, and persistence in living life from a positive aspect.

I would like to give special recognition to my numerologist consultant and dear friend, Michael Bisbiglia, whom I affectionately refer to as Doc Biz. With much of Michael's patient assistance, I was able to bring this book to completion and for this I am truly grateful.

Limitless thanks to my dear friend and teacher, Carla Bonetti. You have inspired me to reach higher just by your way of being. Observing how your life is dedicated to shifting the consciousness of the world and introducing me to people and organizations such as Heifer International reminds me that huge changes are made by one mind, one heart, one action, which can make all the difference in the world.

I thank my friend Michael Anthony, a gifted and talented friend who supported this endeavor, for his undertaking of the editing and his suggestions for this book. I so appreciate your shared unconditional friendship through the years. I love you as a powerful, influential friend and confidant.

Thanks to both my holistic nurse/nun/teacher, Mary Carter, and psychologist Carl Carter; I carry enormous amounts of gratitude for your patience, compassion, and shared understanding of the human body/mind/spirit connection in my early years of bodywork training. How little did I know at the time the impact you would make in my life. I thank you both for being such inspirational role models as well as vessels of wisdom that fed my hunger for truth and knowledge. Yes, Mary, I got Lesson Number 1... Truth is always simple.

I wish to extend my heartfelt gratitude to the karma that brought a life friend and confidant, Anthony Santagati, into my life. I also thank you, Tony, for your encouragement through the years that allowed me to express my passion freely and your support in stimulating my dormant creativity to emerge. It's all good.

To Jacquelyn Aldana, author of *The Fifteen-Minute Miracle Revealed*, I extend my appreciation for the simple reminder in your publications and workshops the power of writing down and focusing on your dreams, goals, and desires while giving thanks as the fuel to creative manifesting.

To my BookSurge professionals—John Rieck, publishing consultant; Angela Johnson, design coordinator; Lauren Woolley, account manager; and Lindsay E. Parker, editorial products manager—I give my gratitude for making my publishing experience as gentle as a spring breeze.

And last but definitely not least, I thank the talented, brilliantly gifted Karen Bleske, who took this project and became the answer to my prayer. I am forever grateful for her commitment and immense support in the editing and publication process. I have been truly blessed to know her and have her in my life.

ADDITIONAL RESOURCES

Aldana, Jacquelyn. *The Fifteen-Minute Miracle Revealed.* Inner Wisdom, 1998.

Braden, Darlene. *What Stops You? Overcome Self-Sabotage: Personal and Professional.* BookSurge, 2006.

Byock, Ira, MD. *The Four Things That Matter Most: A Book about Living.* Free Press, 2004.

Casarjian, Robin. *Forgiveness: A Bold Choice for a Peaceful Heart.* Bantam, 1992.

Dyer, Wayne W., PhD. *The Power of Intention: Learning to Co-Create Your World Your Way.* Hay House, 2005.

Goleman, Daniel. *Emotional Intelligence: Why It Can Matter More Than IQ.* Bantam, 1997.

Hay, Louise L. *Gratitude: A Way of Life.* Hay House, 1996.

Hendrix, Harville, PhD. *Getting the Love You Want: A Guide for Couples.* Pocket Books, 2005.

Hicks, Esther, & Jerry Hicks. *Ask and It Is Given: Learning to Manifest Your Desires (The Teachings of Abraham).* Hay House, 2005.

Ilibagiza, Immaculée. *Left to Tell: Discovering God Amidst the Rwandan Holocaust.* Hay House, 2006.

Linn, Denise. *If I Can Forgive, So Can You: My Autobiography of How I Overcame My Past and Healed My Life.* Hay House, 2005.

Miller, D. Patrick. *A Little Book of Forgiveness: Challenges and Meditations for Anyone with Something to Forgive.* Fearless Books, 2004.

Stokes, Gillian. *Forgiveness: Wisdom from Around the World.* Red Wheel, 2002.

The Secret. [Motion picture]. Prime Time Productions (Producer), 2006, www.thesecret.tv

Tipping, Collin. *Radical Forgiveness: Making Room for the Miracle.* Quest, 2002.

Unity. *Daily Word.* www.unityonline.org/Read_Daily_Word.htm

ABOUT THE AUTHOR

Sunnee K. Roman is a forgiveness consultant with more than twenty years of experience in guiding and assisting others in identifying what no longer serves their highest and best interests. Sunnee uses a unique writing method whereby any person can gain greater self-awareness, clarity, and direction for their lives. Countless people have been empowered, regardless of circumstances, by adopting this simple technique.

Sunnee is also a qualified hypnotherapist incorporating the use of past life regression to get to the root of causes or issues in one's life.

As a licensed body worker, Sunnee uses a technique called BodyTalk, and she wishes to be known as a "body whisperer." Using the technique of BodyTalk she is able to tune into a person's physical body and intuitively translate what the body is saying and wishes to be known at the moment of the reading with her hands-on touch. Clearing and releasing are also common with the hands-on healing work. Her BodyTalk readings are very accurate and she has helped many people with physical challenges in their lives.

For several years, Sunnee has been a catalyst for personal awareness and growth using the ancient art and ritual of fire walking with Spirit of the Eagle ceremonies. In this way, she has empowered people to go beyond what they thought possible, thereby giving them a new sense of confidence to move through any life challenges they may face.

MISSION STATEMENT

My intention is to inspire globally the possibility of greater self-realization through this forgiveness writing process, bringing about transformation and the experience of freedom through genuine and authentic living.

"In the spirit of forgiveness and freedom"

—Sunnee K. Roman

SERVICES

- Private Consultations/Phone Consultations
- Conference-Call Sessions
- Group Workshops